Automotive Compliance in a Digital World

Automotive Compliance in a Digital World

Gilbert L. Van Over III, UBA

Cover design: Molly Ganther

First Printing: March 2018

ISBN 978-0-9989012-1-3

Automotive Compliance Education, LLC
P.O. Box 673
Schererville, IN 46375

Ordering Information:

Special discounts are available on quantity purchases by corporations, associations, educators, and others. For details, contact the publisher at the above listed address, or at www.acecert.org.

While the author and publisher have used their best efforts to ensure the accuracy and currency of the material herein, laws change and we're human. This book is not intended to constitute legal advice, but to provide a basic understanding of some of the most important legal concepts that affect the retail automotive industry. If you need actual legal advice, please seek competent counsel in your jurisdiction (and preferably a member of the National Association of Dealer Counsel, www.dealercounsel.com.)

Printed in the United States of America.

Dedication

To my bride, my soulmate, my rock, Phyllis.

"In a world of temporary things, you are a perpetual feeling."

-    *Sanober Khan*

Table of Contents

Acknowledgements

I listen to the Beatles Channel on XM radio whenever I am driving. This station has an occasional segment where famous or not so famous people play guest DJ to share their four favorite Fab Four songs. Many of them start their segment by saying "This was a tough task to reduce all my favorites to just four." I now feel their pain.

This is my book, and I am not limiting myself to just four, but there are too many people to thank on my journey to name them all.

I'll start with my parents, Gil Jr. and Ruth Van Over. Dad is retired military and holds a Doctorate in History. He taught me discipline and the quest for knowledge. Mom is the hardest working person I ever met who balances that with a great deal of common sense. I don't work as hard as mom, and I am accused of not having any common sense, but I continue to strive to meet mom's expectations.

My wife Phyllis and I are high school sweethearts. We were voted class flirts our Senior (and only year in high school together) year in one of the most rigged elections I know of. She is the social butterfly to my wallflower demeanor.

My children are the triumvirate that every dad would be exceedingly proud of. Penny is the oldest and is married to a great guy in Pat. I feel sorry for him sometimes, but he keeps her grounded. They have two fabulous children, Hailey and Ethan Bell, who bring joy every time I see them.

Nick is the middle child in the Van Over household and married to the perfect girl in Molly. She is like Pat in that she keeps him grounded as well. They have our youngest grandson Mason, who loves to Facetime with grandma to show off the newest word he learned.

Dustin is the youngest of the Van Over kids and is engaged to a wonderful woman Lisa. There is something about us Van Overs, we need soul mates who keep us grounded and Lisa is perfect for Dustin. She has a son Tyler who is a lot of fun to be around.

My mother-in-law Mary Ferrel is an independent, strong-willed woman. A military wife whose husband was overseas for a year at a time fighting the Communists. She held the family together in husband Ray's absence and did a great job raising five children who have carved out their own respectable lives.

I have two departed siblings. My brother Jay was one of the smartest people I ever met. When he was a wee tot, he took a cut off electric cord, an empty spool of thread, some wires, a pencil, and somehow got the spool to spin on the pencil when he plugged it in. He passed away in 2015 from a heart failure.

My sister Pam, passed away in 2017 after a long fight with that insidious breast cancer. In her eulogy, I shared that Pam could not be St. Peter's assistant at the pearly gates in saying yes or no to souls seeking entry into heaven – because she would let everyone in.

My father-in-law Ray also passed away from cancer; his was Multiple Myeloma. Ray was the father-in-law every guy hopes for. He enjoyed sports, had fun bantering, and thoroughly enjoyed his golf. His buddies held a golf outing for him when he retired from the Air Force. He continued that outing annually as an Invitational until his death, open to friends and family by invitation. His children now run a Memorial honoring Ray with donations going to the Multiple Myeloma Foundation.

My brother Vaughn, sister Sheila, brothers-in law Ray, Gilbert, and Chris, and sisters-in-law Kathy, Valerie, and Rebecca all hold a special place in my heart and have each created separate, special memories.

Next up is my crack team of proof readers. Joe Bartolone, Lisa Wooten, Randy Henrick, Ben Fabre, and Penny Bell. They offered outstanding suggestions, corrected typos and grammar, and found more than a few important fact-checks. Thanks team!

Molly Ganther shared her tremendous creative skills in designing the dust cover.

A special thanks to the gvo3 associates who helped me build a nationally recognized compliance consulting firm and supplied many of the war stories contained between the two covers: Joe Bartolone, Penny Bell, Ben Fabre, Greg Oltman, Gary Petty, Mike Ross, Darren Saxton, Harry Saxton, Jamie Taylor, Terry Trottier, and Lisa Wooten.

My mentors helped mold me, and in some cases kept me in line. Most have retired by now and are living the sweet life. Dolce Vita to Tico Alonso, Bill Archer, Mike Bannister, Tom Costello, Dave Ellis, George Halloran, Ernie Hawke, Ceil Michalik, A.J. Wagner, and Kurt Zumhoff. I learned something from each of them and took what I preferred from their management style to develop my own.

Many of our clients delegate the unenviable task of dealing with gvo3 and me as part of the client's Compliance Management System. We would not be nearly as effective as we are without the help of these friends and supporters of our efforts in their dealerships. A special Sláinte to Gary Allgeier, Nick Boicheff, Lori Church, Dan Cirrincione, Wagner Del Aguila, Chris Depperman, Becky Eubank, Holly Goodwin, Steve Greer, Wilson Hudgins, Sara Humbert, Ann Hunter, Paul Germain, Scott Greenhalgh, Ruxandra LeMay, Patti Lindseth, Chris Mackey, Jessica Mattingly, John Malishenko, David Orenstein, Eric Score, Iris Seigel, Josh Towbin, and Melissa Witt. As

Gary likes to tell his new Compliance Officers at our compliance roundtables "Congratulations on your promotion!"

Some of our clients share internal audit resources as great assistance in our compliance reviews. You folks know who you are, and you know how invaluable your help is, but we will keep it our little secret. Thanks for all your great help.

Same goes for all the folks in accounting offices, the Controllers and Accounting Managers, the billers and the F&I Assistants, who help us out by pulling and refiling deal files and paying our invoices!

I've worked with numerous attorneys over the years, and always walked away from a conversation a smarter person. Some of these professionals are clients' counsels, others are industry advisors. They include Kelly Baker, Davis Bauman, Michael Benoit, Mike Charapp, Rob Cohen, Elizabeth Corey, Ed Dawda, Jessica Germain, Jonathan Harvey, Tom Hudson, Richard Ivers, Alex Kurkin, Michael Maledon, Brian Nolen, Terry O'Loughlin, Robert Shimberg, Steve Straske, Shane Spradlin, and Sarah Starkey. I believe they are all members of the National Association of Dealer Counsel (NADC), a trade organization of attorneys who work together to help defend dealers from the Dark Side attacks.

F&I Agents are important advisors and partners to the industry and help many of gvo3's clients with products, product knowledge, and a compliant infrastructure to sell products the right way. Some of the ones I've had the pleasure to work with are Ash Bauer, Randy Crisorio, Troy Good, Arden Hetland, Mike Klass, Larry Pomarico, Charlie Robinson, and Bill Wilson.

Prost! to Jim Ganther and David Gesualdo for giving me the inspiration and whose help guided me through the deadlines to achieve one of my bucket list goals.

Finally, cheers to the many nameless Dealer Principals and Dealership Managers left unnamed in this book who gave me the fodder for some of the war stories.

Foreword

The late publisher, Ed Bobbit, affectionately known as "Coach," initiated numerous highly successful magazines and conferences associated with the automotive industry. In the late 1990's, Coach established the F&I Conference and Exposition where Gil Van Over III, Jim Ganther, and others, including me, were invited to speak on various issues, especially dwelling upon compliance. We were dubbed Coach's "Premier Posse" and continued to support these events by speaking and other provided services. As part of this posse, I became a great admirer and friend of Gil.

I have been the Director of Compliance for Reynolds & Reynolds since 2006, but prior to that, I worked for sixteen years in the Economic Crimes Section of the Florida Attorney General's Office where I primarily investigated and prosecuted car dealers. I shared my experiences and recommendations as part of the Premier Posse at these conferences. My experiences taught me that some dealers were in great need of compliance counseling. Enter, Gil Van Over III and gvo3 and Associates.

Gil was in the vanguard of compliance advisors long before other consultants entered the field. He has over three decades of experience working with dealers regarding their legal obligations concerning financing, leasing, and related issues. He is highly regarded by his colleagues and attorneys in the compliance world and often serves as an expert witness. Needless to add, he is called upon routinely as a speaker at conferences and other events.

All of this makes Gil the right person to write the book you now hold. New technologies trigger the application of other laws creating added legal requirements. No one understands this dichotomy better than Gil.

Automotive Compliance in a Digital World addresses the various issues in the electronic F&I process with a clear underscoring of the various laws which apply. As Gil notes, the electronic dealership cannot cure rogue dealer practices, but it certainly can assist dealers in controlling them. The electronic process provides an electronic history of the transaction so that each facet of the process can be tracked. Dealers who follow the law will find new evidentiary defenses in this technology.

For example, each phase of the e-desking process can be time-stamped and isolated. Less than ethical sales or finance managers will be challenged with this new paradigm thereby protecting dealers from needless regulatory risk.

The book is a practical one as it defines the law in basic terms with real world examples. It is not meant to be a legal or technological text, but a volume dedicated to elucidating most of the compliance issues dealers face now and their technological implications. It should be a welcome addition to every Dealer's and Dealership Manager's reading library.

By Terrence J. O'Loughlin, J.D., M.B.A.
Director of Compliance, Reynolds & Reynolds Company

Introduction

The world is in the midst of morphing from paper to digital and automotive retailers lag behind other industries in this transformation.

We had a head start. The first car deal file was created nearly a century ago when GMAC started financing GM vehicles. The deal file (with two pieces of paper) was likely an envelope instead of the today's two-inch thick file folders.

The processes dealers have implemented in the last 100 years have usually been in response to document compliance with an ever-growing list of Federal Laws, State Laws, and Dealer Laws (dealer policies and procedures implemented to develop a defense against potentially deceptive practices).

This is a guide to help dealers with the tough decision of morphing from pulp to ions, from paper to digital. Many of a dealer's paper-based processes are being successfully converted to digital, including the ultimate storage of a deal file on a server in the cloud instead of walls of locking file cabinets in the Accounting Office.

I refer to a Compliance Management System in the following pages. This is a structured approach to developing, implementing, and managing a compliance initiative and worth your review and consideration.

This guide also walks through many of the higher risk areas the Dark Side attack dealers with and offers up some of the best practices the industry has adapted as a defense to these attacks. Transparency and consistency are the critical keys in creating a Paper and Digital Trail as your best defense witness.

A few words about nouns, pronouns, and the gvo3 writing style.

I will periodically refer to all vehicles as cars. The Paper and Digital Trail I discuss in this book can usually apply to trucks, SUVs, ATVs, boats, motorcycles, RVs, and personal watercraft.

I randomly switch between he and she, him and her instead of picking one gender or using the ugly he/she. When I write that "she is a kinky F&I Manager", that includes all the male F&I Managers.

A few disclosures. I am not an attorney so none of this is to be construed as legal advice. You should consult with your counsel with legal questions. Hopefully your counsel is a member of the National Association of Dealer Counsel and has that great resource available.

The best practices I identify as Dealer Law are implemented after business decisions are made. They are the best practices we recommend when consulting with dealers on how to best develop a defense against Dark Side attacks. If your dealership does things a little different, that is because of your dealer's business decision to apply a different process. Always check with your manager before changing any of your prescribed processes.

The gvo3 writing style sends my word processing grammar check spin endlessly. I'm OK with that because my writing style is closer to how I speak than how my Journalism Professor would grade my papers. I use terms such as "Dark Side" and "BS-ometer". I prefer less formal nouns like "kink", "scam", "ain't", "gonna", or "buddies". I've been writing industry columns for 15 years now with this style, and I ain't gonna change now.

Helping dealers to develop, implement, and manage a CMS for our clients, while they retain or improve their profitability, has been a rewarding career. I've shared my thoughts and opinions in this book and hope you find it enlightening.

CHAPTER 1

Evolving Times Require Evolving Minds

"If something has been done a particular way for fifteen or twenty years, it's a pretty good sign, in these changing times, that it is being done the wrong way."
- *Elliot M. Estes, Former GM President*

Singer Paul Simon rode the pop charts in the mid-seventies with a song titled *Kodachrome.* It extolled the virtues of popular color film and cameras. Buy a roll of film, head to the park or the ballgame, and shoot some pictures. Eventually, the roll of film made its way to a photo shop for developing and printing.

After *Three's Company* had aired a couple of times, one would anxiously pick up the pack of 24 four by five-inch glossies. The disappointment was appalling. The fond memories of the kids with Mickey or the beautiful sunset over the pounding surf became undocumented memories. Most the pictures were out of focus, or someone's eyes were shut, or the lens cap was inadvertently left on. Kodachrome's owner didn't care; you paid for the film, the developing chemicals, and the photo paper.

Then a disruptive technology known as digital technology became more affordable, provided quicker feedback, and by extension, more popular.

This decade, a song titled #*Selfie* emerged on the dance charts. It portrays the current culture of taking selfies with a smart phone, instantly looking at the result, and deciding whether to delete or Snapchat.

Kodak – Business Death Barely Averted

Kodachrome's owner (Kodak) nearly died because its stayed faithful to its antiquated film-based business model instead of moving into the digital era. The inventor of the digital camera in 1975, Kodak ignored its own 1981 internal research, which was driven by Sony's introduction of an electronic camera. The research suggested that digital technology would eventually surpass film, but Kodak had ten years or so to ready itself for the digital revolution. Kodak did not prepare itself, even though it invented the technology, and had ample time to convert its business.

Kodak unfortunately ignored its own history. The Company's founder, George Kodak, had two similar forks in the road with disruptive technologies and took the right path each time. The first time he moved from a profitable dry plate technology to black and white film, then invested in color film over black and white film.

Kodak took the wrong path with its decision on digital technology, and ultimately filed for Chapter 11 Bankruptcy protection in 2012. It emerged from bankruptcy in 2013 a smaller company. It altered its business plan and is now fully engaged in the digital business, still printing photos.

As its internal research suggests, Kodak may have seen the need to morph from analog to digital, but for whatever reason, did not pull the trigger. The photo industry has morphed from an analog business to a primarily digital business. Consumers have greatly improved the development of 4 by 5-inch pictures by using digital technology to screen which pictures to print.

Likewise, dealers who continue to use Sharpies and Four-squares are likely headed toward extinction. Dealers with dot matrix printers are creating potential documentation for litigation because of forms printing offline that dealers with laser jet or e-contracting processes are not concerned with. Refusing to leverage digital solutions for Red Flags requirements because the paper process is just fine…can lead to more identity thefts. It is less likely that a Billing Clerk will print Adverse Action Notices, stuff them into envelopes, stamp, and mail them every single day as opposed to letting RouteOne, Dealertrack, 700 Credit, CBC, or ProMax manage the process.

The overnight digital evolution is not necessarily an overnight event. I recall working on a laser printing and digital solution for dealers in the early nineties. Like the revamping of many processes, there were some roadblocks to clear. For several great reasons, the industry is moving into the digital world.

Defining the e-Dealership

Our industry has been evolving toward the e-Dealership concept, but to this point, everyone seems focused on the e-Process instead of the concept of pulling it all together into an e-Dealership. Perhaps that's the reasoning behind the only reference you will find in Google for an e-Dealership is a Canadian company who uses it to market a fuel system.

An e-Dealership is one that embraces e-Contracting, e-Marketing, e-Storage, e-Etc. For the most part, it is a dealership who has figured out ways to convert pulp to ions. The input and output of the processes are moving from handwritten information on mashed up trees to zeros and ones on a server.

A Call to Documentation

Since Henry Ford introduced the assembly line in 1913 and started mass producing Model T's, the industry of vehicle sales and financing has morphed over time. When GMAC bought the first indirect contract from a dealer in 1919 and created the first deal file, it likely had a title and a contract on one side of a six by eight-inch piece of paper.

Today, a standard deal file contains enough paper to stretch over 75 feet when taped end to end and requires the consumer to sign about 80 times. A dealership manager signs roughly 20 times.

Today's bulging deal file is a call to documentation for the dealer to demonstrate either compliance with state or federal disclosure requirements or transparency in negotiating with the consumer. This call to documentation did not occur overnight but has grown because of political and consumerism zeal to regulate, technology to improve, novel approaches to sue businesses, and people's greed to cheat consumers. Dealers are compelled to document proof that things were done right, or at a minimum, be able to defend themselves against litigation or regulatory oversight.

Some Important Industry Milestones

Here is a timeline of some of the major events over the past century that have taken a deal file from two pieces of paper to two inches of paper.

1913   Henry Ford started mass producing cars – Americans started buying cars.

1914   The Federal Trade Commission (FTC) was created when President Woodrow Wilson signed the Federal Trade Commission Act into law. The FTC's stated mission is to protect consumers and promote competition.

1919   General Motors Acceptance Company (GMAC) started indirect dealership financing. The first deal file is created. Two pieces of paper. Let the analog processes begin.

1920s   Roaring Twenties and Prohibition.

1930s   The Great Depression.

1940s   World War II.

1950s   Korean War, then the Cold War, then Rock and Roll.

Not much happened from an automotive compliance perspective between 1920 and 1957. Americans had other concerns, like food on the table, living through the wars, and partying on either end of this 37-year span. In 1958, however, the Federal regulations started to ramp up and the automobile industry was forever changed and still morphing.

1958   Automobile Information Disclosure Act of 1958, a.k.a. Monroney Act. This Act and the window sticker on new vehicles offered for sale are named after Almer Stillwell "Mike" Monroney, United States Senator from Oklahoma. He sponsored the bill that mandates disclosure of information on new vehicles. There is no truth to the urban legend that the first addendum hit a side window in 1959.

1962   Pat Ryan, known as the Father of F&I, founded the first F&I department at Dick Fencl Chevrolet in suburban Chicago, Illinois. He sold Credit Life and Accident and Health Insurance and did not have to disclose an APR on the contract.

1968   Truth-in-Lending Act (TILA). This law is designed to promote the informed use of consumer credit, by requiring disclosures about its terms and cost to standardize the way costs associated with borrowing are calculated and disclosed. Regulation Z is the Rule the FTC created from TILA. Now Pat must disclose an APR.

1970   Fair Credit Reporting Act. This Act regulates the collection of credit information and access to a consumer's credit report. Its intent is to ensure fairness, accuracy, and privacy of the personal information contained in the files of the credit reporting agencies. Regulation V is the enforcing Rule. This Act also requires an Adverse Action Notice under certain trigger events and circumstances.

1974   Equal Credit Opportunity Act (ECOA). ECOA prohibits creditors from discriminating against consumers based on race, color, religion, national origin, sex, marital status, age, because a consumer receives income from a public assistance program, or because a consumer has in good faith exercised any right under the Consumer Credit Protection Act. Adverse Action Notices are potentially required under ECOA.

1975   Magnuson–Moss Warranty Act – The federal statute that governs warranties on consumer products. One component is the definition of a warranty as coverage that is provided to the customer at no cost to the customer. Ergo…it is a likely violation of Mag Moss to add the cost of a CPO Warranty to the retail transaction.

1976   The Consumer Leasing Act (CLA) was passed to assure that accurate and meaningful disclosure of lease terms is provided to consumers before entering into a Lease Agreement. Regulation M is the FTC Rule governing leases.

1985   Used Car Rule. This Rule requires car dealers to display a window sticker, known as a Buyer's Guide, on the used vehicles offered for sale. The Buyer's Guide was updated in 2017 under the Rule. This is the only Federal Law affecting automotive dealers that I know of which requires a Spanish Language translation of a form if the transaction was negotiated in Spanish.

1990   The Financial Crimes Enforcement Network, or FinCEN, was established to help stem the tide of money laundering.

1994   Summit Systems created and started marketing the first F&I Menu. First envisioned as a sales tool, it has morphed into one of the most powerful documents in a Paper and Digital Trail to prove compliance.

1999   Gramm Leach Bliley Act, a.k.a. The Financial Services Modernization Act of 1999. Among other components of this law, it mandates the handling and protection of consumer non-public personal information. The Privacy Rule and the Safeguards Rule are two of the Rules resulting from this Act.

2001   RouteOne and Dealertrack create the credit application aggregator business, effectively driving away many of the captives' proprietary online credit application systems.

2003   Fair and Accurate Credit Transactions Act (FACT Act) – This law is an amendment to the Fair Credit Reporting Act. The Red Flags Rule is created as part of the FACT Act and deputized automotive dealers and other businesses in the fight against identity theft.

2011   Risk Based Pricing Rule – Under this Rule, dealers must provide consumers with a Credit Score Exception Notice prior to having the consumer sign a contract. California dealers screamed "What took you guys so long?" as state laws in California already required this disclosure.

2011   The Consumer Financial Protection Bureau (CFPB) is the Federale created from the Dodd–Frank Wall Street Reform and Consumer Protection Act. The CFPB brings regulatory oversight and compliance into the digital era as the first Federal created in the internet age.

2013   Congress passes the Military Lending Act (MLA) with a goal of protecting military members and dependents from unscrupulous lending practices. It was essentially a yawn moment for automotive dealers and finance sources until the Department of Defense (DOD) issued a revised guidance in late 2017 regarding the sale of Credit Life, Accident & Health, and GAP to covered borrowers. Hopefully, by the time you are reading this, the DOD has corrected the erroneous guidance and the industry is back to normal.

2017   RouteOne announces that Toyota Financial Services has funded the industry's first remote e-signed contract. The future of an e-Dealership is now upon us.

CHAPTER 2

Traditionalists vs Modernists –
Morphing into an e-Dealership

"If two can be one, who is the one two becomes?"
-     *Daryl Hall and Sara Allen*

My brother in law is an Engineer with a defense contractor. I can't tell you anything more than that...because I don't know. Let's say he takes his Top-Secret clearance seriously and never divulges any more than that.

I could be wrong, but he probably had the first-generation Tandy PC. The one with the cassette tape for memory.

The best way to communicate with him is via e-mail or text. He isn't officially on Facebook but is a suspected FB stalker.

Over the last decade he has purchased or leased four new vehicles. He is agnostic to brand once he settles on the model he wants.

He researches every aspect of his next vehicle lease or purchase online. He knows your cost, the rate from his Credit Union and the Black Book value of his free and clear trade.

He doesn't want to play the Four-Square game and will likely leave your dealership if you try. You can forget acquiring his business if you don't share information with him when he asks for it.

He is the perfect example of a consumer who lives in a digital world. He is a Modernist.

Conversely his mom is on the other end of the analog vs digital continuum.

When one of her kids had a computer tower stored in a spare bedroom, she thought the CD-ROM tray was a cup holder.

She shares pictures and thank you notes by the men and women in blue uniforms who still deliver six days a week. She does not e-mail or text or Facebook. We finally convinced her to upgrade her brick phone to a flip phone, but it is rarely charged or turned on.

Like her son, she has also purchased or leased four new cars in the last decade. She is loyal to brand and dealership.

She would likely walk on a sales person who tried to present numbers or features and benefits on a tablet. She is the living example of a Traditionalist.

Two people from the same gene pool with divergent approaches to the digital versus analog discussion.

My mom and dad live this continuum conflict under the same roof.

Dad is retired Military and has a Ph.D. in History. While we were stationed in Okinawa, he was the Sports Editor for the Pacific Edition of the Air Force Times. Every Spring he buys a spiral notebook. He fills 30 pages with data. One page for every Major League Baseball team. Position players on the top portion, pitchers on the bottom portion. In the top right corner is the name of the home ballpark, its dimensions, and the Manager's name.

Every single day he gets his USA Today or the Lexington Herald Leader, finds the Sports section, goes to the box scores, opens his spiral binder, and logs home runs and RBIs for position players. For the pitchers he tracks wins, losses, saves, and strikeouts.

When I share with him that he can Google that information, or find it on a number of sports websites, he guffaws and goes back to the box scores.

He researched his doctoral thesis at the library and typed it on a typewriter. He remains a Traditionalist.

Mom has a Ph.D. in life. Military families with five mouths to feed usually means the spouse works outside the house to make ends meet. Mom worked in the restaurant industry and put in the bell to bell hours that many dealership managers do. It is difficult to grow up in a household with that type of work ethic and not have some of it run off on you.

Mom was an early adapter to digital versus analog processes in restaurants. She eventually owned then sold two restaurants and usually had the latest restaurant technology instead of paper processes.

She is active on Facebook, sends emails and texts, and knows how to Google for information. She is the Modernist in the household.

Same house, differing philosophy.

Dealerships are struggling with this dilemma...stay analog or switch to digital.

A dealership with a lot of customers like my mother-in-law will likely stay with analog processes and be late adapters to digital.

Dealers with customers like my brother-in-law should probably consider being an earlier adaption to digital.

When mom and dad appear at a dealership, the dealer is probably best served having a hybrid of analog and digital in place.

This battle can be labeled Analog vs Digital, Paper vs Electrons, Traditionalists vs Modernists.

The battle between a Traditionalist and a Modernist is evident in the world outside of automotive retailing. For example, the Modernist is more likely to be a fan of UFC where a Traditionalist still enjoys boxing matches on HBO. The Modernist arranges for a ride-sharing service with an app on her smart phone. The Traditionalist asks the server or bartender to "call a cab". Even pasta is not immune to this battle. The Modernist will go to the local grocery, purchase a box of pasta, a jar of the preferred sauce, and whip them together in the kitchen. In a few minutes – not bad. The Traditionalist, on the other hand, goes to the grocery store, purchases the flour, eggs, salt, tomatoes, olive oil, onions, and garlic. No need to buy the basil, thyme, oregano, or parsley…they are growing in flower pots in the kitchen. Once in the kitchen, the egg is added to the flour, salt added, dough kneaded, then rolled, and cut into the desired pasta. The sauce is put together using an old family recipe and simmers the entire afternoon filling the home with a delicious aroma. Hours later, voila!

Neither approach to life or business is wrong. Each approach has its merits and detractors. It really comes down to personal choices and decisions.

As the sales and F&I processes are morphing from a Traditionalist documentation of the processes to a Modernist documentation, it is helpful to step back to see where the change is taking place.

Benefits and Risks

Each process has its own benefits over the other, and a different set of risks in accepting the approach to use. I'll cover these in depth in another chapter.

For the Traditionalist, employees are already trained in the paper process, controls are in place and it is easier for an absentee owner to oversee the operations. The Modernists believe they are catching the wave now and are meeting consumer demands while building efficient processes. The Modernists also believe a digital process will help flip the consumers' perception of car dealership and the dealer will have easier access to data while having the ability to expand its footprint.

Conversely, staying with the Traditionalist approach means the industry can pass you by, that the consumers' negative perception of car dealers continues to perpetuate, ignoring that millennials prefer digital to pulp, and a larger data storage and safeguards risk. Pursuing the Modernist processes can border on being on the bleeding edge of technology, requires staff retraining, and trying to convert old timers on the new approach. The Modernist must review its controls, backup retention of data, and a risk of a large data breach.

Hybrid

Daryl Hall *(Hall and Oates)* may have said it best when he wrote this classic line in one of the duo's songs, "If two can be one, who is the one two becomes?" My belief is that ultimately, the dealership sales and F&I model may be a hybrid of the Modernist view and the Traditionalist preference.

Some dealerships may have customers who prefer a paper process while other dealers have customers who may insist on a digital approach. This may drive the dealer's ultimate decision.

Further, some processes are better executed using pulp and other processes lend themselves to electrons.

Dealer Processes – Digital or Paper

Here is a look at some of the processes under review by dealerships in their decision between Traditionalist or Modernist:

Credit Applications

Two critical compliance concerns related to credit applications help drive the decision between paper and digital.

First, a dealer must show consent to pull a credit report. While a signature is not required, it is the best evidence to prove permission if the customer signed a credit application. Therefore, in a compliance review, you should review the timing of a signed credit application versus the timing of the credit pull.

The second compliance concern is to be able to prove to a finance source that the credit information you provided is consistent with the credit information provided to you by the consumer. A signed source credit application to compare to the submitted credit application serves as this evidence.

Some dealers are obtaining and retaining a paper credit app signed by the customer while other dealers are accepting an online credit app digitally signed. Other dealers are entering the customer information directly into a kiosk or the CRM and printing a copy for the customer to sign before pulling credit.

All these approaches are compliant.

Desking

Many dealers still using a sharpie and a Four-Square will likely have compliance issues with its desking process. These issues can include payment packing or discriminatory pricing. While some e-Desking solutions can still allow payment packing or discriminatory pricing, it is easier for you to catch it in a compliance audit and know who to hold accountable.

Menu

Like desking, many dealers who use a manual menu and a sharpie may be committing deceptive practices like payment packing or trading rate for product. Using an e-Menu with the industry standards I outline will help with a compliant menu process. It also documents many of the customer's purchase decisions and is the most important piece of paper from a compliance perspective in the Paper and Digital Trail.

Contracting

Truth-in-Lending issues flare up when an impact printer is used to print the contract. Leveraging e-Contracting not only minimizes potential TILA claims, it also helps with contracts in transit funding.

Document Storage

Document storage can be either analog (storing paper file folders in locked cabinets and secure storage facilities) or a digital environment, where all deal documents are digitized and stored on a server in the cloud.

Deputy Dawg Duties

The Federales require auto dealerships to conduct some vetting on each transaction to help in the fight against terrorism and identity theft. These two problems are certainly on many consumers' lists of things to worry about in America and we are required to do our part.

To comply with terrorism vetting (OFAC) and identity theft deterrence (Red Flags Rule), a dealer must check some lists or other data to decide on whether to move forward with the transaction. Trying to manually conduct these reviews is time consuming and likely fraught with errors or omissions. If there are processes within the sales and F&I processes that truly lend themselves to a digital solution, it is OFAC and Red Flags.

Adverse Action Notices

Under this requirement, a dealer sends an Adverse Action Notice as necessary. Many dealers take the conservative approach and send an Adverse Action Notice to anyone who provides a credit application and the dealer does not sell a vehicle to. Manually completing and mailing a mass number of letters is inefficient. A digital approach is really the only way to ensure compliance with this process.

Out of Area Deliveries

This process ties directly into identity theft. Some dealerships are experiencing identity thefts from rings of nefarious, smart criminals. Many of the identity theft cases I've been involved in have some common characteristics and should be considered in your Red Flags process:

- The customer is from out of the area;
- Has never done business with the dealership before;
- May have passed over numerous dealerships for the vehicle; and
- The lack of negotiation over price or products.

Some dealerships have adapted a rather robust process to help mitigate the likelihood of an identity theft from an out of area customer. The process is described in more detail in the chapter on Out of Area Deliveries.

CHAPTER 3

The Genesis of a Compliance Management System

In the beginning, there was General Motors Acceptance Corporation (GMAC) and the emergence of a national indirect auto finance organization. The Treaty of Versailles was signed around the same time, ending WWI. A typical GMAC deal file was the title and a contract too small to fit in today's standard printer tray.

The Federal Trade Commission (FTC) opened its doors around five years before the formulation of GMAC, and by default, became the regulator for the auto and auto finance industry. Its charter was, and remains, to prevent unfair practices in commerce. In 1914, the motivator to create the regulator was to "bust the trusts" that prevailed in many industries. It really gained some power over industry and deceptive practices when Congress passed a prohibition against unfair and deceptive practices in 1938.

That innocuous beginning ultimately begat numerous Federal and State regulations to oversee automotive dealerships. Some folks will tell you that our industry is one of, if not the most, heavily regulated industries in the United States. Jim Ganther is fond of saying "The American retail automobile industry is only slightly less regulated than building a nuclear power plant in the wetlands on top of a manatee eating a bald eagle in Al Gore's back yard."

Jump ahead nearly a century after the FTC's start and witness the birth of the FTC's little brother, the Consumer Financial Protection Bureau (CFPB). The CFPB jumped into our consciousness in 2011 as a reaction to the mortgage lending meltdown. Its charter is like the FTC's charter – to be the consumer's watchdog.

Just like a little brother, the CFPB wants to prove it belongs in the same conversation as its big brother. It was the first federal regulator born in the internet age and leverages the internet in its processes and practices. Through its website, it is an aggressive compiler of consumer complaints of all things financial and logged its millionth consumer complaint in a short five years.

Although the CFPB was unable to wrestle oversight of car dealerships away from the FTC, there is no questioning the agency's intent to regulate dealerships through the wormhole known as the finance sources to whom dealers sell retail and lease contracts.

With regulations come enforcers of the regulations and other opportunists that pursue or influence the pursuit of automotive retailers, each with its own motivation.

Today's Environment

In December 2017, the Department of Defense shocked the auto industry with a revised interpretation of the Military Lending Act. The revised interpretation changed the rules of engagement with regards to the sale of Credit Insurance to certain Military personnel and its dependents (covered member). Credit Insurance is defined in the interpretation as Credit Life, Accident & Health, and Guaranteed Asset Protection (GAP). The sale of Credit Insurance products to a covered member trigger many onerous disclosure requirements, among them the requirement to include the premium as a finance charge in the APR calculation and to ensure that the APR does not exceed the 36% maximum APR under the MLA.

Rightly so, the NADA immediately announced a fight. At press, NADA, and other engaged parties, are working with the FTC and the DOD to find a better solution. Until then, NADA has recommended three options for Dealers on how to operate under the revised interpretation:

1. Suspend the sale of Credit Insurance to covered members;
2. Suspend the sale of Credit Insurance to all consumers; or
3. Continue the sale of Credit Insurance to all consumers and accept the onerous requirements under the MLA.

All our Dealer clients decided to adapt option one or two. Those selecting option two (suspend the sale of Credit Insurance to all consumers) cite the potential of state anti-military discrimination laws which conceivably could apply if Credit Insurance is available to other consumers, but not to military personnel and dependents.

Another option not provided by NADA is to convert the covered member to a lease. Many leases have deficiency waiver protections included within the lease. Other leases permit the sale of GAP on a lease. Either way, a covered member under the MILA will have GAP coverage under this option.

This interpretation was delivered in December 2017, but backdated to October 2016, leaving many dealers potentially at risk for a business practice that was acceptable at the time of the transaction.

In another press release from October 2016, the FTC announced payment packing and yo-yo charges against nine California dealerships, its first such charge levied against an auto dealer for yo-yo transactions. Unconfirmed rumors have the first yo-yo transaction in California in about…oh…1920.

This is an important development for auto dealerships as it signals the willingness of the FTC to accept and adopt some of the CFPB's methods and processes and ideologies.

One potential, very significant future event is the required development and implementation of a Compliance Management System (CMS). The CFPB requires the finance sources it regulates to have a formalized, documented CMS in place. The CFPB Supervision and Examination Manual is a 924-page doctrine that provides guidance for a CFPB examination. Very early in the document is an in-depth discussion on a Compliance Management System and the compliance expectations of any business regulated by the CFPB.

Although the FTC does not require auto dealerships to have a formalized, documented CMS in any area of the dealership's operations, the process is a sound one and makes good business sense. Many industry observers have opined that there is a strong probability that the FTC will adapt a similar requirement to have a documented CMS of all the businesses it regulates, which include automotive retailers.

Overview of a Compliance Management System

A Compliance Management System is the method by which a dealer manages the entire consumer compliance process. It includes both the compliance program and the compliance audit function.

The compliance program consists of the policies and procedures which guide employees' compliance with laws, regulations, and potential litigation defense.

The compliance audit function is an independent testing of the dealer's transactions and processes to determine its level of compliance with consumer protection laws and internal policies and procedures.

The process to develop and implement a CMS is similar with the required components outlined by the FTC in its guidance with the Safeguards Rule and the Red Flags Rule. These components are:

1. Appoint a Compliance Officer;
2. Conduct a risk assessment to gauge current practices vis-à-vis requirements;
3. Develop a policy and procedure manual to address the compliance requirements;
4. Provide and document employee training on the policy and procedure manual;

5. Perform periodic audits to confirm compliance with the policy and procedure manual; and

6. Put corrective actions in place.

How to Implement a Compliance Management System in the Dealership

Assuming the Compliance Officer is named, let's use the Monroney Rule, a rather simple Federal requirement, as an example of how the CMS compliance model would work at a dealership.

Conduct a Risk Assessment

The first task is to understand the compliance requirement. The Monroney Rule requires that all new vehicles offered for sale have a Monroney label affixed to a window.

Now that the requirement is understood, a dealer must conduct an assessment to see how the dealership is complying with this requirement. The logical first step would be to understand the process of affixing Monroneys to the vehicle. Do the vehicles arrive from the factory with a Monroney affixed or is the Dealer responsible for affixing the Monroney to the vehicle before displaying the vehicle for sale? If the Dealer is responsible, what is the process in place to ensure the Monroney is affixed before it is parked on the lot, ready for a new owner?

The logical next step would be to do a lot walk and review the new vehicles for placement of the Monroney label. Are there any new vehicles available for sale without a Monroney? Are there any Monroneys that are shredded because someone rolled the window down during a test drive? Are there any new vehicles with the Monroney in the glove compartment, upside down on the passenger seat, or stuck between the seat and the console? If any of these violations are found, what is the defined process to put corrective action in place?

Develop a Policy and Procedure

Next the Dealer would create a written procedure that explains how the dealership will comply with the requirement to have a Monroney label on every new vehicle offered for sale. In this step, a written policy and procedure would outline the steps to take to comply with the requirement that every new vehicle offered for sale has a Monroney affixed to a window. This document should define the process and identify a responsible party. If the factory normally ships the vehicle with a Monroney affixed, identity the Dealership employee who is to verify the Monroney is indeed affixed when accepting delivery of the vehicle. If it is not affixed, the document should provide instruction on how to order a Monroney and to leave the vehicle in PDI until the Monroney is received and affixed.

Provide Training

Once the playbook is written, it becomes a policy. The fourth step in implementing a CMS is to train the employees on the policy and instruction on the procedures required to implement the policy. This training can be provided in many different channels. The most important takeaway from this step is that the employee understands the requirement and the process. If the regulator audits the CMS compliance, a signed employee acknowledgement is the best evidence a Dealer can provide to prove compliance. An even stronger defense is if you can demonstrate that the employee was trained and passed a test confirming understanding of the material.

Perform Periodic Audits

The CMS is a logical approach to compliance. It is also a logical application in other areas of our society. For example, to build a championship football team, the organization will conduct a review of its roster and preferred playing style. The coaches will develop a playbook of all the plays a team could use during the game. The players spend a lot of time preparing for the game, either in the weight room, the practice field, or film study. Stopping your CMS effort after training employees on how to complete the various processes within the dealership is akin to a football coach to stop managing the game because the training has been provided and the players will respond as trained. Both the auto dealership and the football team are less likely to succeed without a periodic audit of the output of the processes. The football coach has instant feedback through the play and flow and score of the game. The Dealer must schedule periodic inspections of the output of the process flows to ensure the employee is performing the tasks as expected. Using the Monroney process, the Dealer should schedule periodic inspections of the vehicles available for sale to ensure that each one has a Monroney label affixed to a window.

Implement Corrective Actions

The final step in a documented CMS approach to compliance is to implement corrective actions based on the results of the periodic audit. If the periodic audit discovers that five new vehicles are missing Monroney Labels, determine the cause. Did the vehicle come out of PDI without a Monroney attached? Was the vehicle recently test driven and the Monroney was ripped off when the window was rolled down? Once the cause is known, corrective actions can be implemented to reduce the likelihood of the occurrence happening again.

While most successful dealers intuitively use the CMS model to manage the processes in the dealership. They may just not be documenting the approach. The day is likely coming when documenting your CMS will be as important as doing the right thing.

CHAPTER 4

Whose Law Are We Following?

I am frequently challenged in audit recaps, industry presentations, or Letters to the Editor for the magazines I write for when I provide a finding or opinion that something is not in compliance. "Show me in the statute where you have to have a menu" is one common challenge. Early in my career, the recurring challenge was "What law applies to quoting payments?"

In the compliance world, one must test the paperwork, processes, and output against requirements imposed by up to three different laws: Federal Law, State Law, and Dealer Law.

Federal Law

You have heard the age-old axiom that it takes an act of Congress to change something. There is a speck of truth in that statement in the way that laws are passed, and regulations are promulgated. In my terms, this means that Congress passes a law, usually called an Act. Then a federal agency or regulator promulgates rules and regulations pursuant to the Act. The regulator can change the Rule to adjust to current events easier than Congress can change the Act. This is an efficient approach to administering the law that our elected officials intended.

The Gramm Leach Bliley Act (GLB) is an example of Federal Law. There is a statute one can point to and review the compliance requirements. The FTC is the agency responsible for promulgating Rules and Regulations under the GLB, such as the Safeguards Rule and the Privacy Rule. You may recall that in 2013, the FTC modified the safe-harbor template of a Privacy Notice by revising the Rule. It did not have to go back to Congress to revise GLB.

State Law

The state laws essentially work the same as federal laws. The nuances of each state make compliance reviews more than just a 50-state review template. For example, Texas has a disclosure requirement to disclose the trade equity, positive or negative, on a deal. In Michigan, the dealer must check the Secretary of State website for potential repeat offenders who are not eligible to register a vehicle based on past driving or intoxication records. Wisconsin and North Dakota dealers must confirm that the customer does not have a non-Child Support lien. Colorado dealers must execute a DMV Disclosure form with many reps and warranties from the consumer. Minnesota and California have extensive Car Buyer's Bill of Rights disclosure requirements. Some states have usury limits on retail contracts, others do not. A few states require the use of an Implied Warranty Used Car Buyer's Guide, others permit As-Is sales. Wisconsin has its own Used Car Buyer's Guide, separate from the FTC Used Car Buyer's Guide.

Dealer Law

Federal and State Laws are easy to understand. Dealer Law however, is quite different.

Dealer Law is another way of saying we use best practices as a defense against potential litigation or oversight. Often, these best practices have been developed to help defend a transaction against the FTC or State Fraud Act(s) or Unfair and Deceptive Practices Acts.

The definition of an Unfair or Deceptive Practice in Section 5 of the FTC Act is "Unfair or deceptive acts or practices in or affecting commerce." All the states have "Little FTC Acts" that have the same effect as the FTC Act. Quite a mouthful and sounds rather confusing.

Our layman's definition of a potentially deceptive practice is "If it appears confusing, it is probably deceptive."

Other than that vague definition, there is very little specific guidance in these types of acts; just a general requirement to not do it. Thus, the lack of clarity.

Payment quoting methodologies fall within Dealer Law as an approach to help deflect claims of payment packing or discriminatory pricing.

Industry standards have developed over the years as dealers have faced payment packing charges in Oregon and have a payment packing disclosure requirement in California. The National Association of Attorneys General (NAAG) issued guidance in the late nineties discussing acceptable payment ranges, but before the advent of electronic desking systems which eliminates many of the potential variables.

You won't find this in writing in the Truth-in-Lending Act or on the FTC or CFPB website. There is not a national payment quoting law and most states do not have a statute prohibiting payment packing. Prudent dealers who successfully manage risk have identified and implemented an acceptable methodology as Dealer Law.

Remember that time when you were driving down the freeway? On auto pilot, not paying attention to the satellite radio, no text messages to respond to, no driving instructor in the passenger seat reminding you how poorly you drive.

Your mind meanders through a thousand different thoughts, nothing in particular, everything in general. Like observing yourself in a maze from above, hitting dead-ends, turning down a different hall, finding your way through to the destination.

Suddenly, a brilliant idea smacks you upside the head! A new way to improve your processes, your market share, your advertising, your employees' motivation, your whole business model. An enhancement to your business model from an unlikely source.

My recent epiphany is that your F&I and Sales disclosure compliance model should mirror the F&I and Sales processes at dealerships in California. Why California?

Because what is required by statute in California should be considered best practices in the other forty-nine states.

Why California?

According to a few of my fellow consultant friends who specialize in leading 20 Group discussions or profitability training, California dealers maintain higher grosses, profits, and customer satisfaction ratings than the dealers in a majority of the other 49.

One of my past employers saw fit to send this Midwestern boy to Southern California early in my management career. I like to say that I got a decade's worth of experience in my two-year stint. I went there with trepidation. I had bought into the Kool-Aid that California dealers were aggressive to the point of being deceptive. That California dealers were innovative, after all, they perfected the spot delivery process about the same time Mr. Gore invented the internet.

And, a few years after I left, the infamous expose of Southern California F&I Managers going to jail for payment packing ran on one of the national morning shows and put California dealers right next to Washington dealers on the shelf of non-compliant dealers in the public's perception.

What I know now is completely different. California dealers, like most dealers, are bright, driven, flexible, aggressive, adaptable, resilient business people.

When the California Car Buyer Bill of Rights forced disclosure by statute, the dealers used all those qualities to modify and improve their processes. The process changes resulting from new legislation help complying California dealers to have a deal file that can withstand the scrutiny of most deceptive practice inquiries. At least the ones who implemented the improved processes.

California RISC

The same California RISC that enabled dealers to pack payments in the mid-nineties now gives a California dealer its best defense against packing products.

There are three lines to disclose theft deterrent products.

There are two lines to disclose surface protection products

There are five lines to disclose service contracts.

And, of course, a line each for GAP and Credit Insurance (although I do not know of a single California dealership who sells Credit Insurance).

Essentially, the purchase price of the vehicle, optional aftermarket items and every product purchased in F&I is separately disclosed on the RISC. Properly executed, a customer cannot support a claim that she did not know what she was purchasing or how much it cost.

Can you say that about the RISC in use in your state?

Pre-Contract Disclosure

By statute, California dealers (and by Minnesota statute, Minnesota dealers) must execute a form called an Pre-Contract Disclosure (PCD) on every retail financed transaction. On the PCD, the base amount financed, term, and payment are disclosed. Also, on this form is the list of the optional products, with pricing, that the customer agreed to purchase in F&I, including the total amount of the optional products purchased. Finally, there is a disclosure of the final agreed upon payment including the purchased products. It is very clear on the PCD what the payment walk is, and it requires the customer's agreement and signature.

Sounds like a menu to me. Looks like a menu to me. Very definitely establishes a paper trail connecting the agreed upon vehicle purchase price from the sales department to the final transaction documented by the RISC.

The properly completed PCD helps to create a defensible Paper and Digital Trail. A menu in the other 48 can do the same.

Notice to Vehicle Credit Applicant

The Risk-Based Pricing Rule is the final rule created from the FACT Act which passed in 2003. It requires that dealers provide a notice to certain customers with a disclosure of their credit score and where that score ranks amongst consumers across this great land of ours.

Guess what. California dealers had been providing a similar notice for a handful of years before the other 49 and it really is a non-event. In fact, some California dealers tell me it helps to lower some haughty consumers' imaginations of just how good they believe their credit score to be.

In the past, I have put forth the notion that the Federal Sentencing Guidelines, the Safeguards Rule, and the Red Flags Rule provide a good compliance model for dealers. I still maintain that thought.

The California disclosure model fits nicely into an overall compliance model for compliance with Dealer Law.

Examples of Processes Subject to Dealer Law

I stopped in the local fast food joint last week. The one with the fabulous lemonade. Don't ask why, but I needed three gallons of lemonade.

"May I help you?" the young lady behind the counter asked.

"I'd like to have three gallons of lemonade," I responded.

"Will that be for here or to go?" she asked without hesitation. I simply smiled, she stopped for a few seconds, then said, "Yeah, I guess that will be to go."

While I waited for the young man to fill up three gallons, the place got busy. The young lady behind the counter stayed with the word tracts she had shared with me. Even though the place was getting crowded quickly, her training and her word tracts helped her to manage the surge of business.

The busier you get, the tighter your processes must be. Dealers who implement sound policies and processes are able handle sales surges.

If the CFPB or the FTC comes knocking and they follow their compliance investigative playbook, here's their play. They will be asking a dealer about its policy manual, how it was developed, and how it fits into the dealer's overall compliance program. Well operated dealerships will be able to answer these regulators' questions. Many Dealer Laws will be noted in the policy manual. The Federale may just say "Thanks" and move to the next dealer target.

Payment Quoting Methodology

For dealerships that quote payments during the sales process, this Dealer Law will outline the approach to developing the first pencil. The intent for this Dealer Law is to provide a plausible defense against potential claims of payment packing and discriminatory pricing.

Two possible conditions exist before the first pencil is quoted, either the credit bureau report has been pulled and the credit score is known, or the credit bureau report has not been pulled and the credit score is not known.

If the credit score is known, the payment quoting methodology should use an APR based on a rate matrix. Here is a sample rate matrix:

Bureau Score	New (60 Months)	Used (CY – 3) (60 Months)	Used (> 4) (36 Months)
> 700	Captive BR + 2.50	Captive BR + 2.50	Captive BR + 2.50
650 – 699	Captive BR + 2.50	Captive BR + 2.50	Captive BR + 2.50
600 – 649	Captive BR + 2.50	Captive BR + 2.50	Captive BR + 2.50
< 600	Captive BR + 2.50	Captive BR + 2.50	Captive BR + 2.50

The bureau score is in column one, the next three columns contain the APR to be used depending on the bureau score. For example – a customer with a 735 bureau score and a captive finance source's buy rate is 3.00%. The first pencil will be calculated using a 60-month term and a 5.50% APR (captive buy rate plus 2.50%)

The bureau bands and reserve markup are arbitrary in this sample: each Dealer should use the template and develop its own rate matrix.

The Dealer Law key is to consistently use the rate matrix to calculate the first pencil.

In the event the bureau score is not known before quoting the first pencil, develop and consistently apply an average rate on every first pencil. There are a few schools of thought on the development of an average rate, all of which are appropriate provided the rate is used consistently. Some of these approaches include:

- Computing an average rate from the last 90 days of contracted sales. Most dealers who use this approach will eliminate any subvened rate deals from the calculation. This requires monthly monitoring and can be labor extensive;

- Using the captive's level two buy rate plus standard markup. The average credit score in America is a 687 score, which normally falls within the level two rates at most captive finance sources; or

- Selecting an arbitrary rate and using it consistently. Some dealers will use 6.00% for new and 9.00% for used. Other dealers will use 8.00% for both new and used. Still other dealers use state max (typically dealers with most of its business with subprime customers).

Dealer Law will dictate that this methodology will be used on all transactions. The key to compliance is to apply this methodology consistently.

Menu Usage

You will not find a federal or state statute that requires the use of a menu during the F&I process. Menu usage is very simply a Dealer Law requirement.

Menus did not originate in auto dealerships. Both of my Mom's restaurants used menus to allow diners to make informed choices. It listed the entrees available and gave a brief description of the entrée along with the price. The menu was divided into lunch selections, dinner selections, daily specials, drinks, and sides (or options). Given these choices, the diner might have some clarifying questions for the server, but ended up making an informed choice, fully aware of the costs that were adding up.

The restaurant or fast food menu approach is like the menus at auto retailers. Most menus give the purchaser the information to make an informed decision on F&I products purchases. A more extensive discussion on the industry standard that has evolved regarding the menu is undertaken in another chapter. At a minimum, the menu must demonstrate that the customer was aware of the payment with and without F&I options, term, APR on a retail deal, products selected, products declined, and price of selected products.

Accepting Credit Applications

Some of the components of the credit application process is covered by federal and state laws, specifically those statues prohibiting bank fraud, and the requirements for pulling a credit bureau. The remaining requirements are Dealer Law.

These Dealer Laws are intended to provide defenses against claims of not having permission to pull credit, bank fraud, and recourse demands from finance sources for providing misleading credit applicant information during the credit decisioning process.

There is a wave of consumers with less than desirable credit scores who have turned to companies promising to clean up their credit with a resulting higher credit score. In most credit scoring algorithms, the number of inquiries can reduce a credit score. These companies encourage the consumers to fire off letters to all creditors whose inquiry shows on the credit bureau report stating that the creditor did not have permission to pull credit and demanding that the inquiry be removed.

Another factor at play is the Dealer-Lender Agreement that Dealers must sign before submitting contracts to any finance source. These Agreements contain representations and warranties to which the Dealer agrees. While the language will vary slightly, every Agreement I have read contains a basic requirement that the Dealer will provide true and accurate credit applicant information during the credit decisioning process. The finance sources are vetting the five key credit determinants to affirm that information the Dealer is submitting meets this standard.

Dealer Law should mandate that the consumer sign a credit application giving the dealer permission to pull credit and the Dealer will retain a copy of the signed credit application. This application can be a handwritten credit application, printed from the Dealer's CRM, or be submitted through any one of the available online portals.

This policy will potentially provide a defense against claims of not having permission to pull a credit report to recourse demands citing inaccurate credit applications. I am aware the statute does not require a signature to pull credit, it only requires that the dealer has consent and a permissible purpose. Most dealers take the belt and suspenders approach to obtain a written signature on a credit application before pulling credit as proof of consent.

Product Pricing Guidelines

Some states have statutory guidelines on some F&I products. Every state regulates the pricing of Credit Insurance (Credit Life and Accident & Health). Some states regulate GAP premiums. Florida does not regulate pricing on service contracts, etch, or tire and wheel, but the product provider must file the rates for these products and the Dealer must sell it for the filed rate. In all other instances, Dealer Law must prevail.

The reason for a Dealer Law in product pricing is to avoid the possibility of price gouging by an overly aggressive F&I Manager. Many times, we see prices that can be considered exorbitant by industry standards, and too often the consumer is a member of a protected class. In other words, the lack of an acceptable pricing policy can lead to claims of discriminatory pricing.

Additional Used Vehicle Considerations

Federal law requires that every used vehicle available for sale must have an approved Used Car Buyer's Guide prominently displayed on the vehicle. If the deal was transacted in Spanish, a Spanish translation version of the Guide must be provided. California, Colorado, and Florida are among the states that require a prior history disclosure.

Other issues germane to used vehicles are building in the industry. Recalls have become problematic because of availability issues. Prior damage or usage can become the genesis for a complaint.

Dealer Law must provide the process requirements to help with a defense against these types of claims.

Many dealers are using sources such as CARFAX, Auto Check, Safercar.gov, or NMVTIS to vet for prior usage or damage. Most dealers will also share that the information is not necessarily current as it can take some time for prior damage or recalls making their way through the system.

Dealer Law in place at many dealers is to print a report from whichever source it uses on the date of delivery, have the customer and dealership manager sign the report, give the customer a copy, and retain a copy of the signed report in the file. The Manager is also instructed to use a word tract like "To the best of our knowledge, this is the prior usage, history, recall, or damage information available today, the day you are taking delivery of the vehicle".

Military Lending Act Confusion

The Military Lending Act is a federal law. It was passed in reaction to some unscrupulous people who took advantage of young, enlisted Military personnel. The Department of Defense provided its interpretation of the Act so that finance sources and Dealer who sell and finance vehicles to Military personnel understood their requirements.

Well – in December 2017, many moons after its initial interpretation, the DOD issued a revised interpretation, and made it retroactive to October 2016. This revised interpretation created confusion, angst, and conflicting guidance statements.

The MLA or the revised interpretation only requires a creditor make certain disclosures to covered members (Military personnel and dependents) if Credit Life, Accident & Health, or GAP is sold.

Most industry experts recommended one of three options for Dealers: Don't sell credit insurance products to all consumers; don't sell credit insurance products to covered members; or sell credit insurance to covered members and make the appropriate disclosures. I add the ability to convert the covered member to a lease, as the guidance appears to apply to retail transactions.

For the Dealers who decided to stop the sales of credit insurance to all consumers, no additional Dealer Law applies.

For the Dealers who decided to sell credit insurance to covered members (and I am not aware of any), the disclosure requirements are Federal Law and no Dealer Law is needed.

For the Dealers who decided to continue the sales of credit insurance to consumers, but not to covered members, a Dealer Law is required. The DOD provided a website for Dealers to check to confirm whether the consumer is a covered member or not. The finance sources who purchase contracts from Dealers are also checking this website and will likely bounce a contract if the correct disclosures are not made.

Dealer Law under MLA processing is to check the DOD website on all customers before starting the menu process. If credit insurance is sold, the printout of the website must be retained in the file.

Dealer Participation

As a summary, the CFPB pursued some of the finance sources that Dealers do business with alleging that the finance sources were guilty of discrimination in the way Dealers managed the dealer participation process. Using a questionable approach and a flawed methodology, the CFPB extracted millions of settlement dollars from the finance sources.

The finance sources then turned their sights on Dealers by using the same flawed methodology to suggest to Dealers that their portfolios with the individual finance source exhibited signs of discrimination.

In response to the response, NADA provided an industry guidance based on a consent decree between a Pennsylvania Dealer and the FTC. Essentially the guidance requires the Dealer to establish a standard rate participation percentage, then document the reason for closing the transaction at a lower percentage mark-up.

The CFPB does not require Dealers to adapt this process, nor does the FTC. The Dealers who did adapt the NADA guidance did so to have a plausible defense for the eventuality of potential finance source allegations. Dealer Law.

Smart Dealers Establish Dealer Laws

One of the intents of Federal and State Laws is to protect the consumer against nefarious people. Smart business people will leverage Federal and State Laws to provide protection for themselves by complying with the laws and retaining the documentation to prove compliance.

Smart Dealers also develop and implement certain Dealer Laws to provide direction for their managers in those areas where the Federal Law or State Law is either silent or confusing.

The Dark Side Defined

"Fear is the path to the Dark Side."

- *Yoda*

In a hit movie from my youth, two bandits are being pursued across the Old West and Mexico by the Federales. At one point, just before going down in a blaze of glory, one bandit looks at the other one and asks, "Who are those guys?"

I can imagine the same conversation going on between dealers at meetings where dealers commonly get together to chat about the state of the industry. "Who are those guys?"

I affectionately lump them together in a group I call the Dark Side. These are the entities that are pursuing car dealers with an overabundance of regulations, exposure, and oversight to further their own agendas and motivations.

Keeping with the movie analogy, I have fun in my articles and presentations by using the *Star Wars* Dark Side terminology as an analogy for the forces that attack the Good Side dealers.

Perhaps the first thing I need to say about the Dark Side is that not every plaintiff attorney or attorney general is a card-carrying member of the Dark Side. The Dark Side I refer to are the folks who attack car dealers with unfounded or frivolous lawsuits or inquiries or exposes, not the honorable lawyers, attorneys general, television stations, or bloggers who pursue truly unscrupulous businesses.

The Federales

Motivation – Consumerists at heart, protecting the charter of government protecting citizens.

The first team member of the Dark Side is by far its most active. These include the Federal Trade Commission, (FTC), the Consumer Financial Protection Bureau (CFPB), the Department of Justice (DOJ), the Internal Revenue Service (IRS), state Attorneys General, and state Divisions of Motor Vehicles (DMV) among others.

As the genesis of the FTC pre-dated the industry's first national captive finance source, GMAC, by five years, it ultimately became the primary overseer of dealership business practices. Ergo the FTC Used Car Rule, the FTC Safeguards Rule, etc. This is the agency that is leading the fight against identity theft, telemarketers, deceptive advertising, and consumer fraud.

The CFPB jumped into our consciousness in 2011 as a reaction to the mortgage lending meltdown and the passage of the Dodd Frank Act. The CFPB's charter is like the FTC's charter – to be the consumer's watchdog. The CFPB is the first federal regulator born in the Internet age and is an aggressive compiler of consumer complaints of all things financial. It logged its millionth consumer complaint in October 2016, a short five years after its formation. Its claim to fame so far has been the millions of dollars it has extracted from the finance sources we do business with in the name of disparate impact. The agency has a new Director as of November 2017. He revised its mission statement to perhaps reflect a changed approach to its regulatory perspective. The new mission statement reads:

"The Consumer Financial Protection Bureau is a 21st century agency that helps consumer finance markets work by regularly identifying and addressing outdated, unnecessary, or unduly burdensome regulations, by making rules more effective, by consistently enforcing federal consumer financial law, and by empowering consumers to take more control over their economic lives."

Time will tell.

The DOJ is where the Federal Bureau of Investigation (FBI) resides and is led by the U.S. Attorney General. It is responsible for the enforcement of the law and administration of justice. The FBI is the one who investigates the potential crimes and has been active in potential bank fraud cases.

The Internal Revenue Service (IRS) and Financial Crimes Enforcement Network (FinCEN) lead the Federales fight against money laundering and the Bank Secrecy Act.

State DMV offices have varying authorities beyond the issuance of vehicle titles. Some have enforcement authority and can be active investigators of consumers complaints against auto dealers.

Attorneys General (AG)

Motivation – Some say consumerists at heart, pessimists contend simply looking for votes.

Some believe the acronym AG is a metaphor for Aspiring Governor. These politicians need votes to continue their political careers and the Attorney General office is perceived as a stepping stone to the Governor's mansion. Most see an effective approach to garner votes is to aggressively pursue bad businesses in their state that take advantage of consumers.

We can applaud the AG who goes after the scam artists who are stealing money from senior citizens or the traveling band of roofers who leave leaking tops on houses. Just don't pursue an upstate dealer with a two-year inquiry that had no merit to begin with. Don't post misleading brochures on your website comparing car dealers to mortgage brokers and calling the mortgage brokers the honest one.

Plaintiffs' Bar

Motivation – Pursuing a Major in Money, a Minor in Consumerism.

It seems there are too many attorneys for too little legitimate litigation. Do an internet search for "Attorneys, name of town where you live or work). Then do a search for (Car Dealers, same town). Regardless of your map coordinates, your search will likely have more results devoted to attorneys than it has devoted to auto dealers. Dealers are outnumbered!

The Plaintiff's Bar remains as active as ever. The National Consumer Law Center (www.nclc.org) is a highly organized organization of plaintiff's attorneys. On its website, one of the first opportunities I must review, or purchase is a report on "Auto Add-ons Add Up: How Car Dealer Discretion Drives Excessive, Inconsistent, and Discriminatory Pricing." This same organization publishes several how-to-litigate-car-dealers' manuals. Some working titles are *Consumer Warranty Law, Unfair and Deceptive Acts and Practices, and Automobile Fraud.*

The *Unfair and Deceptive Acts and Practices* is over 1,000 pages long and tackles such topics as what to look for in discovery (recap sheets, faxbacks, deal files, and paper trail), uncovering hidden dealer assets, F&I products, and sales processes. It then lays out how to litigate the case, and finally, what to expect as a settlement. Some of the practices they claim as potentially deceptive include unwinds, yo-yo transactions, selling the trade too early, lack of disclosing prior use or damage, misrepresenting a lease as a retail transaction, and many more.

Local Media

Motivation – Ratings for the station, stardom for the anchor.

As much as I rail against the media for being empty heads and pompous asses, you'd never suspect that my first collegiate major was in the School of Journalism.

I was taught to vet every part of my story with three independent sources. Now, a single unnamed source appears sufficient. Now it is "The person whose life we are destroying with this story did not immediately respond to our messages for a comment." I wonder how much time the target was given to respond. Five minutes?

During sweeps month, somewhere, some dealer is going to get lambasted with a highly emotional expose alleging that the dealer unfairly dealt with a consumer or five. You can expect to see word bites from sympathetic "victims", files containing hundreds of pages of paper thrown on the desk and a look at a "secret" internal document alleging that the dealer screwed the consumer(s).

Think about some of the big profit deals you've had lately and how it would play on the local news. For example – "Local dealer sells Catholic priest $11,000 of unwanted insurance" or "Area senior citizen walked into a local dealership to buy a battery and drove away in a new luxury car."

Unfortunately, the dealer is often powerless to respond. The Dealer Principal cannot go on camera and say, "Well, the reason the consumer paid 28 percent interest was because the consumer had a 310 credit score, has never paid anyone in his life, did not have any money to put down, was $5,000 upside down in his trade that was not running, and had just started a new job." The dealer never has an opportunity to defend itself in the court of public opinion. The dealer can only say, "If it happened, we will take appropriate action" and hope the adverse public opinion does not close the business.

Kinks

Motivation – Baffling at times. Can be narcissism, can be alcohol, drugs, or gambling.

Kinks defy a short definition, so I had to devote a full chapter to them. Keep reading!

Social Media

Motivation – Some would say a need for attention, others would say a quick path to #FakeNews.

My friends Mike Charapp and Rob Cohen, both esteemed dealer attorneys, define social media as "The term 'social media' refers to platforms and networks where users have the opportunity to exchange messages, photos, videos, and opinions on their experiences."

We monitor a few industry related social media chat groups. In one post, a finance manager was extremely upset over a scenario at his dealership that day and posted it on an online forum. The conflict was with a sales manager and the topic was whether to deliver a potential straw purchase. The finance manager was adamant that the deal not go through while the sales manager was just as adamant that the car start moving down the road.

Not only do dealers need to monitor and honestly react to consumers lodging complaints on the many social media outlets, but dealers must also manage the company's expectations of employees' use of social media in either denigrating or promoting the dealership.

The dealer's website requires constant monitoring. Many Federales consider the website to be advertising and hold the advertising claims on the website to the same standards as print, radio, and television advertising. Bogus reviews on the dealer's website are fodder for potential misleading or false advertising claims. That same FTC we discussed earlier settled another case with a 12-store dealership group in Los Angeles in late 2017. The dealer agreed to pay $1.4 million because of violating a prior consent decree on advertising practices.

Preventative Medicine

So, what's a dealer to do to defend itself against the Dark Side? Unfortunately, there is nothing anyone can do to prevent from being sued, pursued, litigated, or regulated. There are, however, some steps a dealer can take to limit the likelihood of a Dark Side attack.

With so many moving parts, unless you want to erect the Great Wall around your dealership, you must focus on the process. The best way to protect your dealership and yourself from the Dark Side is to have an effective Compliance Management System in place.

Establish a tone from the top. These types of acts will not be tolerated and will lead to disciplinary action, including termination.

Handle complaints when they start and don't let them escalate into lawsuits. Most of the lawsuits I work on as an expert witness start as a complaint of some sort not related to the complaints in the lawsuit. The infamous lawsuit on backdating contracts in California started with a customer claiming he was promised upgraded wheels.

Establish processes, policies, and procedures that mandate full disclosure in sales and F&I. Document that the consumer made informed decisions at each step in the process.

Establish working relationships with your regulators and local media. Most regulators want little problems to go away. They will appreciate the opportunity to call you and get a complaint handled rather than move forward with an inquiry. Most local media are looking for legitimate stories and will move on if they call you with a complaint and you handle it instead of stonewalling them.

Someone in authority must oversee the overall compliance program. Call this person the Compliance Officer. Make sure everyone knows who your dealership's Compliance Officer is.

Conduct a risk assessment of your processes using federal and state requirements or best practices as your benchmark.

Develop and implement a policy and procedure manual to outline how your employees are expected to execute each part of the process. Develop and implement policies and procedures for Safeguards, Red Flags, Social Media, Sales, and F&I. Provide the materials to all involved employees and obtain an acknowledgement to adhere to the policies after the employees have sufficient time to review the materials.

Establish a list of non-negotiables that, if violated, warrant immediate termination. This list should include any form of bank fraud or criminal activity.

Train and test your employees on your policy and procedure manual. Then train and test them again in six to nine months. Then update your policy and procedure manual and train and test them again. Then do it again.

Require that your employees be certified with an independent industry certification like Automotive Compliance Education (ACE). ACE requires the annual, continuing education certifications that the top trust factor occupations require.

Regularly audit the output of the process to confirm that it is compliant with your policy and procedure manual.

Regularly review your policies and procedures for modifications as new technology, regulations or efficiencies evolve.

CHAPTER 6

Kinks Will Be Kinks

"Think of how stupid the average person is and realize half of them are stupider than that."

- *George Carlin*

During our increasingly less frequent family functions, we frequently like to play cards. Growing up military, bridges were blown up, not played. Instead, we play Rook. Or Hearts. Or Uno. Or Euchre.

It doesn't matter which family or which game; the players can be divided into two camps. Most us are in the play by the rules camp. A minority needs to be watched as they love to stretch, bend, or obliterate the rules. We in the majority know we can't fix kink, but after all, they are family, so we keep them around. We know we can't change them; we watch them closely.

In our business, though, we don't have to keep the kinks around.

During exit conferences with Dealers, we can categorize our findings into one of three types: Naïve, Sloppy, or Kinky.

The first category is those issues that are caused by being naïve. By not understanding what the compliance requirements are.

The second category is being lax, being lazy, being sloppy. The dealer and the managers know what the requirements are and have policies and procedures in place to comply, they just don't execute them consistently.

Being naïve or being sloppy can be corrected through training or motivation.

The final category is caused by being kinky. Once a kink, usually always a kink. The only cure is to kick the kink from the organization.

Being Naïve, Lax, Lazy, Sloppy

Being naïve, being lax, being lazy, being sloppy creates their own special set of issues.

For example, when a deal is started in the dealership's computer system, it is assigned that day's date. If the vehicle is delivered on a subsequent date, or the deal is recontracted later, the DMS does not always update the date. If the F&I Manager does not change the date on the deal, all the documents are effectively backdated. This can cause potential Truth-in-Lending violations or possible incentive qualification issues.

The reasons for these potential issues is that that the F&I Manager either did not know to change the date (naïve), was in a rush to get the deal completed (lax), or just didn't feel like doing it (lazy). Being lax or lazy constitute being sloppy.

The fixes are to either provide training so that the F&I Manager knows better or provide motivation so that the F&I Manager knows she better.

Kink Is a Kink

I attended an event at a football stadium. The line to the Men's restroom wound out the door as guys patiently waited their turn to use one of 19 urinals or five stalls. Ironically, there was not a wait to use the four sinks. This recurring theme has always made me shake my head with bewilderment. So much so that I conducted an informal, unscientific survey of washroom attendants when one was available.

Since then, I've been at nine different venues where a washroom attendant is offering a towel in return for a tip. The consensus of these nine attendants is that most guys do not wash their hands after using the facility.

Some of these restrooms had paper towels. Others had upgraded to environmentally friendly air driers. A few had both.

It takes more than new technology to change behavior. If you are a guy who is not inclined to wash your hands, it won't matter what the drying method is. If you are a guy who carries hand sanitizer or makes sure to wash hands after every use, you will use paper or electrons, whichever is available.

My conclusion? Updating to the newest technology won't necessarily modify behavior.

Being a kink creates its own special set of issues.

Kinks and Bank Fraud

A finance source rep recently lamented about the number of buybacks the institution was faced with and the strain it was putting on the relationship with dealers. At this institution and many like it, the recovery department scrutinizes the credit application for violations of the dealer-lender agreement when an account defaults. Most of the buybacks were a result of the dealers misstating the income on the credit application.

Sometimes the income was simply increased. Other times the customer had two jobs and the dealer represented the total income from the two jobs as one income from one job. Other times the customer's occupation was changed from self-employed to manager and the customer's small business went under.

The finance source representative shared that the responses she received amazed her when she asked why the income was wrong. The most honest answer was "I know what your payment to income ratios are and I had to adjust the income to fit the deal to your guidelines."

A kink will give the customer a raise or a promotion when transferring the credit application information from the source credit application to RouteOne or Dealertrack.

A kink will lie to the bank about how the subcompact car grew a moonroof.

A kink will falsify the amount of cash down payment on the contract so that the transaction fits within the lender's underwriting guidelines.

A kink will knowingly orchestrate a straw purchase.

These kinky acts constitute bank fraud. Bank fraud is a crime. When an employee commits (or tries to commit) bank fraud, the dealership's name is listed on a secret Suspicious Activity Report that the finance source is required to file with the Federales.

Other Kinky Acts

A kink will tell your customer that the lender required a GAP policy. By requiring an F&I product, a kinky F&I Manager is violating the federal Truth-in-Lending Act if she does not include the premium in the APR calculation. Too many of these situations could create a class action lawsuit against the dealership.

A kink will start the menu with a base payment calculated at 12% when he has a 6% buy rate in hand. Once price or payment objections surface, the kink will magically be able to call in a favor at "the Bank" or use some coupons from "the Bank" to bring the payment with products in line with the customer's acceptance level. The deal ends up at 8% and the customer never knows what the true base payment was or what the actual payment walk was.

A kink will increase the final sales price of the vehicle from the original agreed upon amount using deceptive fees, taxes, or charging twice for addendum items.

A kink will pack the payments using artificially high interest rates, excessive days to first payment, decreased months per year, including undisclosed products in the payment, using an undisclosed short term such as 24 or 30 months, or just simply adding $25 worth of leg to the payment quote.

These things that a kink will do can put the dealer and dealership in harm's way.

I don't profess to be an Human Resource expert, and you should probably consult with yours before brooming a kink, but I really don't see any other way to fix kink. There have been numerous instances where we uncovered a kink at a client, and the client rid itself of the cancerous kink. Shortly thereafter, we conduct a review at another client in the same city, who has hired this kink, and we find the same issues as before.

If you are prone to power book a deal to meet the finance source's callback or underwriting guideline, you will continue to manipulate the options on the book-out sheet, either paper or transmitted through a credit application portal.

If you view credit application fraud as a victimless crime, you will continue to give people raises or stability or move them back in with their family instead of paying rent. It does not matter that you are now committing potential bank fraud using the internet.

If you are a kink, having e-processes won't change your behavior…it only makes it easier for people like me, or the dealer, or the Federales to figure it out.

A kink has a faulty moral compass.

You just can't fix kink.

e-Processes Leave an Electronic Trail

e-Processes are a huge benefit to the Dealer Principal who intends to run a transparent and compliant e-Dealership.

While a kink can still pack payments using an e-Desking system just as easy as if she were still using a Sharpie and a Four-Square, the e-Desking system tracks the history of the pencils. Using an e-Desking software, I can tell what the first pencil is and if it is compliant with the dealership's desking policy. I can tell if the manager had a credit approval in hand and quoted a payment more than the credit approval's max rate. I can tell if the number of days to first payment or the number of payments per year were manipulated to pack the payment.

In fact, it is easier for me or a member of the Dark Side to verify that the payments are packed when an e-Desking software is used. This is a huge benefit for the Dealer Principal to understand who is following the dealership's desking policy and compliance training and who the rogue kink is.

Those Who Object

Ofttimes when a dealer is trying to convert from pulp to electrons, some of the sales managers object and create barriers to implementation. I can tell you from experience, I find a higher percentage of payment packing at dealerships who still employ handwritten Four-Squares than those dealerships who have converted entirely to e-Desking.

What Did a Kink Want to Be?

I was listening to the Beatles Channel the other day and listened as the DJ shared a personal story. Seems he was a Beatles fan growing up and completed a sixth-grade project discussing the legitimacy of the "Paul is dead" rumors. I thought "This guy knew he was destined to become a Beatles expert when he grew up and fulfilled his dream".

Then I thought about the interviews with little kids who share they want to be Firemen or Police Women or Doctors or Nurses when they grow up.

Which leaves me wondering…what did the kinks in our business want to be when they were little? Did they spend time figuring out how to cheat at hop scotch and convert that to packing payments on Four-Squares?

People who dreamed of being a kink when they grow up and fulfilled their dream will not change their behavior because of e-processes. It will only make it easier to catch them.

CHAPTER 7

The Paper and Digital Trail –
A Dealer's Best Defense Witness

"It's amazing how many cheaters and liars believe they won't be caught. News Flash: In today's age of technology, there won't just be a paper trail. There will be multiple electronic and digital trails, as well."

- *Cathy Burnham Martin*

Consumers can lie!

"Just let me take care of it," the man at the next table demanded of his companion. "It will be free."

He then called the waiter over and started loudly berating him because the steak was cold, they were in a rush to make the play, and the service was lousy. Finally, the manager made her way to the scene and after a short conversation agreed to comp the dinner with profuse apologies. As the couple left, I swear I detected smirks on the couple's faces.

When we arrived at the restaurant, the couple was already seated and happily chewing away on their medium rare steaks.

We finished our meal discussing the gall of someone to look for a free meal and headed to our play. To our surprise, the couple was at the same play.

To recap – they smiled while eating a medium rare steak then complained it was cold. They smirked while leaving the restaurant in a rush to make the play, then waited close to an hour to gain admittance to the theater.

Consumers do not always tell the truth!

I spend a little bit of time helping defend dealers who get involved in litigation. The customer is alleging that the dealer has wronged him or her in some way. In case after case we can make a logical argument that the customer was not completely up front with the dealership during the transaction and had the truth been known, the dealer would likely not have gone through with the transaction. And if the dealer would not have gone through with the transaction, there would not be the basis for a lawsuit. Many attorneys refer to this as the "Dirty Hands Doctrine".

So, how do you protect yourself against less than honest consumers? Not an easy question to answer, but here goes.

Many of my cases as an expert witness involve subprime consumers. There are a couple of theories as to why subprime consumers are more likely to be less than honest with dealership personnel. One theory is that they are desperate to obtain financing and will provide or manufacture whatever stip you need to get the deal funded. We have identified several websites that promise to provide fake stips. Paystubs, utility bills, social security cards, proof of insurance, and Credit Privacy Numbers (CPN) which are marketed as a nine-digit number to replace the Social Security Number.

Another theory is that they are subprime because they are usually looking for shortcuts in life and often fail.

The misinformation we've leveraged in past cases to demonstrate the dirty hands doctrine include falsified credit applications and manufactured proof of income.

To offset this risk, your managers must take the time to vet the documentation provided. If the decimals do not line up on the pay stub, it might be manufactured. If the time at address is listed as five years, yet the driver's license was issued six months ago and has a different address, it might not be right on the credit app.

Other cases though, involve prime customers who, through a review of the evidence, are making false claims to try to get a free lunch. Prevailing theories on these types of cases is that there are just some people in this world trying to get something for nothing. Or perhaps they are just filing lawsuits to try and extract a settlement to go away. Or, heaven forbid, a plaintiff's attorney needs work!

The best defense in these types of cases is to have the facts on your side. My Law 101 professor constantly drove home the point "If the law is against you, pound the facts. If the facts are against you, pound the law. If the law and the facts are both against you, pound the table."

Your attorney can best defend you if the paper or digital forms in your deal are properly executed and supports the fact that you have negotiated and consummated the transaction in a transparent and compliant fashion.

Like it or not, some consumers are looking for freebies. Sometimes we need to slow down, make sure we have the documentation correct, and ultimately protect ourselves against the consumers looking for freebies.

Is Slipping Tranny a Truth-in-Lending Claim?

I once provided litigation support for a dealer in a case that ultimately settled before the facts were tried by the judge. This claim started as a service complaint about a slipping tranny but had morphed into a Truth-in-Lending lack of disclosure claim.

The plaintiff's attorney was one of the sharper ones. It was obvious in all the other depositions in the case that he was going after dealership employee's credibility.

The sales person involved in the transaction testified in his deposition he no longer worked for the dealership. In fact, he had held numerous jobs in the two years since he quit after one month selling cars. His current job of laying concrete involved as little mental gymnastics as he evidently put into his sales position.

He also conceded that he had no clue what Truth-in-Lending or other federal or state laws were, and that the dealership had not provided any training in closing a deal. The numbers did not match from document to document. The file was missing a menu, a Privacy Notice, a Credit Score Disclosure Notice, and a few other documents the dealer insisted were required on every deal.

This small dealership did not have an F&I Manager. It was the Sales Manager's responsibility to close deals, but he testified he was too busy to close this deal. The Sales Manager delegated the close to the inexperienced sales person to review the Truth-in-Lending disclosures and explain to the customer why she was signing 80 times.

To quote *Pretty Woman*, "Big mistake. Big mistake."

I wasn't privy to the strategy discussions between the dealer, his attorney, and his insurer that led to the decision to settle. I suspect the damaging deposition testimonies and lack of a documented Paper and Digital Trail may have played a part.

The dealer might have had a fighting chance if the deal file had a documented Paper and Digital Trail which demonstrated the consumer was making informed choices at each step of the process. Or that anyone spinning a deal received the proper training. The dealer didn't, and the Dark Side won.

In another one of the lawsuits I helped a dealer defend against had a memorable exchange between the dark side attorney and the salesperson on the deal.

Attorney: "Tell me, Mr. Salesperson, do you remember selling my client his car?"

SP: "Yes, I do. And I know I did everything right."

Attorney: "How many cars do you sell a month?"

SP: "Fifteen to 20. And we always do things legally."

Attorney: "And you sold this car three years ago?"

SP: "Yes."

Attorney: "So, in the three years since you sold my client his car, you've sold maybe 500 or 600 cars?"

SP: "Sounds right."

Attorney: "And you remember selling my client his car?"

SP: "I sure do. And we did everything legally."

Attorney: "What color shirt was my client wearing?"

SP: "I don't know."

Attorney: "Was it raining or was the sun shining?"

SP: "I don't remember."

Attorney: "What did you have for lunch that day?"

SP: "I dunno. Maybe a burrito from the Roach Coach?"

Attorney: "Was there anyone with my client when he bought the car?"

SP: "Ummmmmmmmm."

Attorney: "How can you really sit there and tell me you remember this deal when you can't even remember anything else about that day?"

Case closed. As soon as the salesperson admitted that he could not recall any other details about some deal three years back, the rest of his testimony was tainted. He thought he was helping the dealership defend itself in the lawsuit, but instead created a headache for the dealer's attorney.

In an industry that asks its customers to sign their names on paper or digitally at least 80 times from meet-and-greet through delivery, a consistent documentation process is indispensable. Dealers are tweaking their sales and F&I processes and insisting on documenting agreements between dealer and customer that meet state and federal guidelines, protects car buyers, and can serve as an unimpeachable witness in case of an enforcement action.

We affectionately call this documentation *The Paper and Digital Trail.*

e-Desking	e-Menu	A/D	Digital Buyer's/ Lease Order	e-Contract RISC/Lease	Enrollment Forms

A defensible Paper and Digital Trail takes care of most of potential compliance concerns arising out of a dealer's variable processes. It documents the agreed upon sales terms, demonstrates a consumer knew the payment walk, obtains an agreement to arbitrate differences, commits the consumer to reps and warranties, and finalizes the financing or lease arrangements. That's a mouthful and it is intended to take the wind out of the Dark Side's blowhard arguments.

In most states, a best practice Paper and Digital Trail starts with a final sales agreement, whether on a clear and concise e-Desking worksheet or a printed preliminary Buyer's Order. It continues to a menu, preferably an e-menu, and an Accept/Decline page affirming products purchased. Then on to a final Buyer's Order, moves to the retail or lease agreement and concludes with enrollment forms for all products purchased in F&I.

I know – here he goes talking about forms again. But it is not just having the forms, it is having the forms executed properly to support a transparent transaction.

Think about it, a typical F&I Manager will process 75 transactions each month, or 900 deals a year. Depending upon when the lawsuit is filed, that is an awful lot of transactions to try to sort through and remember the specifics of the transaction. The manager can't be expected to remember the transaction and should readily admit that he does not remember the particulars of the deal.

The F&I Manager must testify to the dealership's processes and policies and procedures. She should outline the way deals are done, describing the paperwork and electronic forms the dealership uses to negotiate the deal, and the transfer of information on the deal from sales to F&I. She must tell a jury that "I process nearly a thousand deals a year. This deal was three years ago. I don't remember the plaintiffs or the deal, but here is how I do things."

A competent defense attorney will then draw out the process and show that the paperwork and digital forms in the specific transaction supports the testimony.

Here are some general rules of best practices to ensure that the execution of the Paper and Digital Trail helps to defend challenges to the transaction.

It's a match!

The numbers must match. It must be clear to the six jurors in the box, whose math skills vary from guzintas to statistics, whose reading pleasures range from comic books to Shakespeare, whose musical tastes may include rap and classical, that you didn't hide anything when you sold the vehicle. Some in the industry lament the fact that a contract is not a contract. It would be so easy if we could just rely on the Buyer's Order, retail contract or lease agreement to support the transaction. Unfortunately, we don't necessarily live in a logical world.

When the firm that eventually became known as GMAC started financing vehicle purchases for General Motors' customers nearly a century ago, a deal file consisted of a one-sided agreement and the vehicle title. There was no APR disclosure. No arbitration provisions. No Seller's Right to Cancel agreement. One signature and the customer financed the new purchase.

Through a combination of greed, hungry plaintiff's attorneys, politicians disguised as Attorneys General pining for votes, and the Federales protecting the unaccountables, times have moved forward from the simpler days of a contract being a contract.

Today, a customer essentially endures a mortgage closing with paperwork sometimes hastily gathered in fifteen minutes. A properly completed Paper and Digital Trail will document the agreement to purchase products, at the same price, on every Paper and Digital Trail document. Leveraging laser printing or e-contracting enhances the likelihood that the documents are completed properly and speeds up the process.

It's about time!

Most of today's dealership systems software enables anyone to track the date and time that Paper and Digital Trail documents are created and printed. Not only do the Paper and Digital Trail documents have to mathematically match, it must be demonstrated that they were executed in the proper sequence. It does no good to have a menu timestamped three days after the date of the contract.

When the Dark Side challenges a dealer about potentially deceptive sales practices, the defense must be the dealership's process, not the testimony of the F&I or Sales Manager. The F&I Manager must testify that he doesn't remember the deal in question but knows his process. I then get on the witness stand and testify that I reviewed 100 deals the F&I Manager spun before and 100 deals after the transaction in question. If the facts support it, I will be able to testify that the F&I Manager followed Dealer Law in these 200 deals.

If the date and time stamps do not support the process, the logical Dark Side question is, "If your process is to sell F&I products using a menu, why is the computer-generated time stamp dated three days after the date of the contract?" In other words, how could you have possibly used a menu to sell products if it was printed three days after the contract?

The Paper and Digital Trail defense is blunted if this occurs.

It's her signature!

Consumers sign around 80 times on a standard deal to complete the transaction. In the Paper and Digital Trail documentation, the customer must sign each document in every place the document calls for a signature. Some

Retail Installment Sale Contracts can require up to eight signatures. Some state forms can require initials in ten spots.

If a document is not signed, or heaven forbid, denoted by "Signature on File", the Paper and Digital Trail starts to crumble.

It's a mulligan!

Dealers who spot deliver vehicles will invariably have transactions that they guessed wrong on and cannot convince a finance source to purchase the paper as structured. In those instances, the customer is called back in to sign again. Sometimes the terms of the new deal are considered detrimental to the customer and can lead to charges of a yo-yo transaction. This is a high-risk area for private litigation and regulatory oversight. The Paper and Digital Trail on these transactions must be perfect.

A recontract must be viewed as a new transaction. As an expert witness, I want to be able to say the previous transaction is void so that any mistakes made in the prior transaction are corrected in the recontract.

In those states where permitted, a recontract should start with a rescission agreement or acknowledgement of rewrite. Collect the old docs from the customer and mark them void, obtaining the customer's signatures by the void notation.

A recontracted deal continues with a new menu, even if the base terms have not changed. Then, in order, a new Buyer's or Lease Order, a new retail or lease agreement, and finally, new product enrollment forms.

A final note, on retail financed transactions, all the dates on the newly executed forms must be the date of signing, not the date of delivery. Failure to do so is another potential Truth-in-Lending violation.

It's check-in time!

Pilots flying prop planes or jet airliners and everything in between, regardless of the number of hours logged, use a pre-flight checklist, and concede it is a mundane task at best. However, every single pilot I've ever chatted with admit they conscientiously complete a checklist before every flight, because they know it can mean the difference between life and death.

Using a post-closing checklist to confirm you've completed the transaction correctly and to your policies and standards is mundane at best. Conscientiously completing a checklist affirming all Paper and Digital Trail documents were properly executed and signed can be the difference between winning or losing a lawsuit.

It's a match – product prices must be consistent on all signed documents.

It's about time – date and time stamps must support the process flow.

It's her signature – over 80 signatures, all required.

It's a mulligan – recontracts must be viewed as brand new transactions.

It's check-in time – use a checklist before billing deal.

Follow the Paper and Digital Trail best practices recommendations and hopefully you can parry the Dark Side's inquiries.

Compliance Enforcement Platform

DealerSafeGuardsSolutionS (DSGSS) offers a digital enforcement platform where the dealer sets the policies and procedures for the first eight steps on the Road to the Sale. It will gather consumer and transaction information at each step of sale and create a digital credit application that is pushed to RouteOne and Dealertrack.

The power of the software is that a sales person or manager cannot move to the next step in the process until he or she satisfies the current policy and process, eliminating shortcuts, rogue behavior, or unintended errors that could potentially lead to problems.

Every time an employee steps out of bounds, based on the rules engine set up by the dealer, an alert is immediately sent to the designated manager or owner to notify them to the misstep. The platform links the dealerships policies and procedures with the intended sales process and people, creating a single, consistent, compliant Road to the Sale.

Since this is a paperless process, DSGSS creates a digital deal file of the documents created and signed by the consumer during the first eight steps to the sale leading up to the F&I turnover. For example, Privacy Notices, credit apps, We-Owes, Payoff forms, Borrowed Car Agreements, would be in the digital deal file. An employee can add additional paper documents such as subprime stips or Red Flags clearing documentation to the digital deal file. This digital deal file can then be exported into Reynolds & Reynolds DocuPAD digital deal file or CDK's digital deal jacket or any other third-party scanning system.

CHAPTER 8

Suspicious Activity Reports and Dealer-Lender Agreements

"The jig is up, the news is out, they've finally found me."
- *Tommy Shaw – Styx*

I was once in a Chevrolet dealership when a customer came in and wanted the dealer to deactivate his vehicle's OnStar feature. His reason? Since the Federales owned part of General Motors, he didn't like the idea of the Federales being able to track his comings and goings through OnStar.

Similarly, I constantly hear stories of customers who become nervous nellies when they discover that you will file the required FinCEN 8300 report with the Feds. There seems to be a not so peaceful, uneasy feeling when dealing with reports of our activities to the Federales.

Suspicious Activity Reports

Perhaps, unknown to you, there may be reports being sent to the Federales naming your dealership as participating in bank fraud on a regular basis, and you don't even realize the reports are being submitted.

A federally insured institution is required to submit a report ominously named a Suspicious Activity Report (SAR) whenever a transaction smacks of bank fraud. Further, unlike the 8300 report that requires you to notify the person you submitted a report on, the institution is prohibited from notifying you that an SAR was filed. Just as equally unknown in the industry is that dealers are also required to file an SAR if they suspect unlawful activity such as laundering of drug money. Not doing so could lead to a SAR naming the dealer.

It is important to remember that the Federales are serious about ferreting out bank and mortgage fraud.

I am aware of an institution in the Southeast that was under the SAR scrutiny. This institution was required to hire a bevy of retired Federales to conduct an audit of every transaction covering a period of time. These retired Federales spent most of a year poring over every transaction and filing a SAR every time it was required. The institution paid a fine for every filed SAR and paid the Federales a nice daily consulting fee and travel expenses for the privilege. Refusal to do so meant the institution would lose its charter.

Dealer–Lender Agreements

I hesitate to use the term Dealer–Lender Agreement because Dealers do not sell contracts to Lenders, they sell them to Finance Sources. The moniker Finance Source is technically more accurate than Lender, like a Service Contract being more technically correct than a Warranty. But the Agreements themselves usually contain this verbiage and this is what the industry knows them as.

Let me also make this disclaimer. While many of the agreements in place have similar reps and warranties that an owner obligates its dealership to, there may be variations from finance source to finance source. You should read every agreement in place with every finance source to understand specifically what you have agreed to. For example, some agreements state that it is a violation of the agreement to use a third-party check guarantee service, remedied by contract repurchase. Other agreements are silent on this potential requirement.

These agreements are in place for every dealer with every finance source the dealer sells paper to. I am not aware of any finance source who will buy the first contract without this agreement in place. The reason is simple: the dealer is agreeing to many reps and warranties that will guide the contractual relationship between the dealer and the finance source. It provides the finance source with certain remedies, such as contract repurchase, if the dealer violates any of the reps or warranties.

Here are some of the typical reps and warranties contained in a Dealer – Lender Agreement that are commonly cited as a reason for a dealer to repurchase a contract or reimburse the finance source for a portion of the credit loss:

Credit Information

"Any credit information supplied by Dealer or to the Buyer is true, complete and accurate to the best of the Dealer's knowledge."

Case study: Growing up as an Air Force brat, I was fortunate to live in some exotic places. There was Rantoul, Illinois; Wichita Falls, Texas; and Honolulu, Hawaii, to name a few. I was further fortunate to spend some of my high school years in the islands. While there, I sampled some of the local cuisine, like papayas, mangos, and poi. I miss the papayas. I miss the mangos. I don't miss the poi. Good poi is hard to find. Even in the islands.

Good POI (proof of income) is sometimes as equally hard to find at some dealerships. Apparently, some dealership managers don't understand the ramifications of manufacturing proof of income for a finance source to support the lie that the finance source relied upon to approve the deal. Unfortunately, like the dealer who lost a wrongful termination lawsuit from a former (and now present) employee who forged some documents, I must categorically state that manufacturing stips is not permitted. The dealer lost the lawsuit because the policy manual did not state that forging documents was not permitted. I'm not making that mistake here.

Other dealers accept POI from a customer at face value. Unfortunately, there are numerous websites available to consumers that promise to provide fake POI and other common stips needed for credit approval. For example, for the low price of $49.95, you can purchase a software program that will "Produce professional quality proof of employment/income for anyone anytime!" Dealership managers must vet all POI and other required stips for legitimacy. If you question one, simply forward it to the finance source for approval before delivering the vehicle.

Make sure the POI is one acceptable to the finance source. Many will list eligible POI sources in their underwriting guidelines that you can find in RouteOne or Dealertrack. An example from one of the finance sources is "Pay stub, W-2, tax return, bank statements, standard Social Security Administration benefit/award letter, or letter from employer verifying consumer's income (on official company letterhead).

Here are some steps you can take when reviewing POI:

- Decimals line up correctly in pay stub columns;
- Year-to-date field should foot from prior pay period;
- Totals in the "current" field should foot;
- FICA and Medicare deductions are correct;
- Consumer name is spelled correctly;
- Consumer address is consistent with address provided on credit application;
- Employer address is consistent with address provided on credit application;
- Verify that the phone/address a consumer provides for employer information is different from the personal references;

- Proof of income documentation is created in a professional accounting-based program, or printed from the company's URL (not www.myfakepaystub.com) as opposed to an Excel spreadsheet or Word document; and
- Letter from employer verifying proof of income should be printed on official company letterhead. Do not accept a proof of income letter from a consumer that is not official in nature.

Down Payments

"Dealer shall collect all amounts due from the Buyer in full as a down payment pursuant to a Contract purchased by [finance source] hereunder in the form of check, cash, or certified funds prior to [finance source's] purchase of the Contract."

Case study: An Attorney General recently levied fines and restitution worth $150,000 against a dealership for a "litany of deceptive acts." The list of allegedly deceptive acts comprises a significant percentage of compliance no-nos, including: deceptive advertising, signing blank contracts, stuffing products, promising rate reductions, holding documents until funding, and increasing the cash price to offer discounts.

Straw Purchases

"A straw purchase means the origination of a Contract by a Customer on behalf of another who is not a party to the Contract with the intent of providing such party primary use or possession of the related Vehicle and where such Customer intends that party to make the payments owed under the Contract."

Case study: This news flash was not published in the conventional news media, but rather in one of the online forums I periodically lurk on. The poster, an F&I Manager, was extremely upset over a scenario at his dealership that day. The conflict was with a sales manager and the topic was whether to deliver a potential straw purchase. The F&I Manager was adamant that the deal not go through while the sales manager was just as adamant that the car started moving down the road. The sales manager kept pushing the "we're all here to sell cars" theorem while the F&I Manager valiantly resisted with the "I ain't doing the perp walk for anyone" argument. In the end, the General Manager did not take a position, leaving the F&I Manager out to dry.

Power Booking

"The Vehicle and all options therein are accurately described in the Contract... the Buyer's order submitted to [finance source] for each Vehicle accurately reflects the items purchased, all options and the terms and conditions of such purchase, and Dealer has not misrepresented the description or any of the terms and conditions of such purchase"

Case study: My second job in this business was as a management trainee for one of the domestic captives. The first step as a management trainee was the collection desk, working the phones and beating the streets to collect the deals our credit analysts put on the books. As a metrics driven company, each employee had numbers driven performance objectives. Meeting these objectives would mean higher performance review ratings, which meant bigger raises and quicker promotions. One of my performance objective metrics was credit losses due to repossessions and charge-offs. The smaller the loss, the better my performance rating. Power booking would exaggerate the amount of the credit loss. The first time I approached my supervisor with a case of power booking and requested that we ask the dealer for a check for the missing options, I learned a very important lesson. "We will overlook this one because it is a loyal dealer and we don't want to risk future business over $500." This was the general opinion in the lending industry oh not so long ago. Today, it couldn't be further from the case.

Take the case of the General Manager who is spending up to 20 years in federal prison without parole, plus a fine up to $250,000, and an order of restitution. The fraud he admitted to? Power booking leases over a four-year period for over $60,000. What was he thinking? Obviously not clearly. All the leases were with the same leasing company. Any good leasing company will check the options that were represented on the vehicle at the time the lease is approved and booked with the options that are on the vehicle when the customer terminates the lease and returns the vehicle. Power booking a lease not only increases the advance and potential pay plan enhancement for the manager, it also increases the residual value. This leads to a lease turn in going to auction, commanding a lower price, and increasing the credit loss to the lessor.

Since a violation of any of these reps or warranties is a violation of a dealer's agreement with the finance source, by extension, it is bank fraud. This triggers the SAR reporting as federally insured finance institutions are required to file the report in instances of bank fraud.

It does not matter when the institution discovers the alleged fraud, whether it is a straw purchase discovered during collections, or power booking is uncovered when the vehicle is repossessed, or falsified income becomes evident during the customer interview process. It does not matter if there was intent by the dealer the dealership manager to commit the fraud.

About the only sure way to know that an SAR has been filed is when the lender either kicks a contract during funding because of bank fraud issues or asks for a check or buy back when the car is repossessed.

The essential point is this: If a federally insured institution receives a contract from you that has evidence of bank fraud, the institution will report the transaction on an SAR. Enough SARs and the regulator may turn the case over to the Department of Justice and FBI. Just ask the ghost of Louis Harrelson.

How to Protect Yourself

To protect yourself and your dealership from being named on an SAR, you must implement a policy and follow-up to ensure compliance.

Consider these steps:

- Establish a policy that bank fraud is a prohibited practice and will not be tolerated;

- Require that all managers read the policy and sign an acknowledgement form that also includes the statement that violations of this policy could result in immediate termination;
- Develop processes to document compliance;
- Require that a manager sign each used car book-out sheet verifying options. Require a signature even if the Manager's name appears at the bottom of the book-out sheet. We've seen occurrences of managers sharing passwords and you will want to eliminate that excuse. This will help limit power booking;
- Regularly audit the income listed on source credit applications to income submitted to lenders via RouteOne, Dealertrack, CUDL, or other online credit application portals;
- Watch for multiple pieces of proof of income documentation from the same employer. This may indicate a dealership employee is creating pay stubs to meet the stipulation requirements;
- Look out for different types of proof of income documentation for the same employer within multiple deal jackets. This also may indicate a dealership employee is falsifying pay stub information to meet stipulation requirements;
- Beware of a trend with the use of the same company name, phone number, or address as an employer;
- Be suspicious of recently prepared tax returns for prior years;
- Repossess all the bottles of white-out or cases of correction tape. White-out marks on proof of income documentation are usually problematic;
- Thoroughly review documentation provided to finance sources to satisfy their stips as a conditional approval. A PDF file can be altered using the PDF Editor function. Look for different fonts or inconsistent information;

- Have the dealership's IT department run a scan of your system looking for pay stub templates or Social Security award letter templates that may have been created by a dealership employee;
- Confirm the down payment receipts match the down payment disclosed on the retail contract or lease agreement;
- Raise awareness in the dealership to straw purchases. Many straws can be uncovered by billing clerks prior to submitting the package to the lender; and
- Require that anyone in the dealership aware of the bank fraud must report it or they are just as complicit in the fraud as the primary perp.

e-Desking

e-Processes are a huge benefit to the Dealer Principal who intends to run a transparent and compliant e-Dealership.

As the industry is moving from manual processes to digital processes in varying degrees, the desking process is one process that is ripe for digitization…perhaps even at the top of the list of the processes that should be converted.

Working Theories

We have a few working theories in our consulting practice. These working theories help us to focus on probable areas of concern as we begin reviewing deal files. One working theory is that if a dealership is still buying Sharpies to complete paper Four-Squares, we will probably find a higher percentage of packed payments or potentially discriminatory pricing. That is if we can fully decipher the scrawl and figure out if the green Sharpie is the first pencil or the final agreement. If we can't decipher the scrawl, and three sales managers cannot agree what the final agreement is, it is a safe bet that the Dark Side will present the Four-Square as a deceptive sales process.

At the least, we usually find that there is not a consistent approach to quoting the first pencil.

This working theory was partially validated, albeit with an incredibly small sample size, by an article that references a recent "undercover" investigation by the National Fair Housing Alliance.

This article discusses the undercover investigation of eight dealerships selling seven brands in eastern Virginia that concluded that nonwhite consumers were offered less favorable credit terms than white consumers, even when the nonwhite consumer had more favorable income or debt to income ratios. Although the report has too small of a sample size to legitimize the findings, it illustrates why perfect adherence to a dealer's first pencil matrix is so important. A similar Dark Side expose can happen to any automotive retailer without its knowledge

A dealer's best defense is to do business uniformly, based on the consumer's credit score, and according to an established matrix.

There are two primary sales processes in the industry today. Some dealers will not quote payments during the sales process and focus on negotiating the trade difference before TO'ing the customer to F&I.

Other dealers employ a process where the focus is on the payment from very early in the sales process. Some dealers use a combination of the two.

Compliance Pitfalls in Desking Deals

Focusing on the sales process where payments are quoted, there are many compliance pitfalls that a dealer must guard against. Working the trade difference is not as susceptible to compliance issues...after all, if you don't quote a payment, you can't pack a payment.

The first potential compliance issue with quoting payments is an expectation from the Dark Side that the payment quote is accurate for what is disclosed and contemplated at that point in the negotiation. One of the members of the Dark Side, the Attorneys General, coined the phrase payment packing around 30 years ago and consider it a deceptive practice.

Payment Packing.

This can take many forms, such as including undisclosed F&I products in the payment quote, using an undisclosed short term to artificially increase the payment, using a rate that is higher than the known rate if an approval has already been obtained, extending the number of days to first payment, or shortening the number of payments per year. Of course, the old-school ubiquitous LEG is packing a payment.

It can be difficult to detect some of these methods with a colorful, confusing Four-Square. Maybe that is why some Sales Managers or GSMs insist on keeping the paper forms and buying stock in Sharpies.

Discriminatory Pricing.

Another problematic issue with quoting payments can be perceived discriminatory pricing. If I conduct an analysis of the first pencils during a period, and the results show that any of the protected classes under the Equal Credit Opportunity Act were quoted higher rates that the rest of the deals, an allegation of discriminatory pricing could be leveled.

As was the case with one Southern California General Manager. I was having a casual conversation with him in his showroom before beginning the file review. I asked him what his desking process looked like. Without a smirk, he pointed to a non-Caucasian female and said, "I can tell you what her credit score is without pulling a credit bureau, so that is how I pencil deals." He was serious, and the review of his deals supported a potential case of discrimination. The white guys were quoted lower rates on the first pencil than were the females and non-Caucasians.

Compliant Desking Process

Many dealers who quote payments during the sales process have implemented a policy on how first pencil payments are to be quoted. Essentially, it depends on whether the credit score is known or not.

If a credit bureau has not been pulled, the Dealer Law requires that an average rate be used to quote the first pencil. The average rate can be the rolling 60 or 90-day average APR (less factory subvention deals). This requires ongoing calculation, maintenance, and communication as it must be calculated each month.

Another approach is to take the captive's buy rate for a 687 credit score and add an allowable mark-up, such as two or two and a half points. The reason for using the buy rate for a 687 bureau score is that a 687 bureau score is the average bureau score in America. This average is also available by state, so the average bureau score for your state can be used to determine your average rate. For example, Minnesota tops the list with an average credit score of 718, while Nevada is number 50 with a 660 average bureau score. A 718 bureau score is likely a tier one score at your captive, while a 660 score is usually means a tier three buy rate. The Nevada one was a bit of a surprise, so I asked an unnamed source for his take:

> "There's lots of construction, lots of jobs in the hotel industry that are not "great paying" housekeeping, food workers etc. or involve people who get paid weekly and cash their checks at casinos. Schools don't pay well and when the economy busted a lot of people let homes go back.
>
> Throw on top of that a lot of vice habits with video poker bars on every corner and the temptations gambling brings and the results lend to people getting overextended."

If a credit bureau has been pulled, a published rate matrix determines what rate must be used on the first pencil.

Bureau Score	New (60 Months)	Used (CY – 3) (60 Months)	Used (> 4) (36 Months)

> 700	Captive BR + 2.00	Captive BR + 2.00	Captive BR + 2.00
650 – 699	Captive BR + 2.00	Captive BR + 2.00	Captive BR + 2.00
600 – 649	Captive BR + 2.00	Captive BR + 2.00	Captive BR + 2.00
< 600	Captive BR + 2.00	Captive BR + 2.00	Captive BR + 2.00

Additional policy requirements include the disclosure of term, no more than 45 days to first payment, always use 12 payments per year, do not include undisclosed F&I products, do not add LEG, and keep the payment spread on the first pencil to $5 or less.

e-Desking

Uncovers the Kink

While a kink can still pack payments using an e-Desking system just as easy as if she were still using a Sharpie and a Four-Square, the e-Desking system tracks the history of the pencils. Using e-Desking software, I can tell what the first pencil was and if it was compliant with the Dealership's desking policy. I can tell if the manager had a credit approval in hand and quoted a payment more than the approval's max rate. I can tell if the number of days to first payment or number of payments per year were manipulated to pack the payment.

In fact, it is easier for me or a member of the Dark Side to verify that the payments are packed when e-Desking software is used. This is a huge benefit for the Dealer Principal to understand who is following the dealership's desking policy and compliance training and who the rogue kink is.

More Professional Presentation

Presenting a consumer with a printed pencil from a computer system is a more professional presentation than green, red, blue, and purple Sharpies on a form that has been photocopied so many times many of the words appear to be of another language. Add the hokey smiley faces to the Four-Square and the dealer risks losing credibility with some consumers. Most consumers, who do not trust car sales people to begin with (remember that survey from an earlier chapter?), view the schlocky Four-Square with colorful Sharpies as a confirmation of, not a repudiation of, that lack of trust. It is tough to keep continued rapport if the consumer does not trust you.

The professional presentation of each pencil, provided in a logical sequential order, that affirms the negotiation at each point of the road to the sale, has better optics for the consumer fighting to overcome the stereotype of the car sales person.

Promotes Consistency

The e-Desking software available today can load a rate matrix and a default rate into the software. If a credit bureau report is pulled, the first pencil rate defaults to the pre-loaded rate matrix. If a credit bureau is not pulled before the first pencil, then the system uses the default APR to calculate the first pencil quote. If the manager does not override the defaults, then the first pencil will be provided in accordance with the dealer's first pencil methodology.

The absolute key to a compliant desking process is that the process is applied consistently and documents when and why a manager deviates from the policy. Any dealer serious about improved desking processes will convert from the analog approach of using Sharpies and Four-Squares to the digital dealer's use of e-Desking software.

e-Menu

It is difficult to find a document in the Paper and Digital Trail that helps a dealer with its compliance story more than the menu. When a menu is properly executed, it affirms the agreement in sales, clearly sets out that the products selected in F&I are optional, fully discloses the payment walk, and closes the F&I sale. One process, two pages.

Unfortunately, either through kinkiness or naivety, an improperly completed menu, usually a manual or paper one with Sharpie assistance, can document a litany of declared deceptive practices. These can include payment packing, confirming the packed payment from sales, stuffing products, or trading rate for product.

Menu Best Practices

California and Minnesota require a Pre-Contract Disclosure (PCD) on retail deals that is the closest statutory requirement we have for anything resembling a menu. The PCD does not disclose the APR and is only required on retail financing, leaving leasing, outside lien deals, and cash deals without a requirement to provide the disclosure.

The PCD does require the base and final payment, the products selected, and the price for products. One of gvo3 & Associates' clients successfully petitioned the Minnesota Attorney General's office to accept the Accept Declination page from its menu process as a substitute for the state required PCD.

In the other 48 states, there is not a statutory requirement for anything resembling a menu. Most retailers have adapted the use of a menu as a Dealer Law, both as a sales tool and a compliance tool.

Through the years of evolving menus and menu presentations, a few best practices have evolved as industry standard.

Industry standard is a coveted standard to be able to apply to a process when I provide litigation support for a dealer. It tells the Dark Side that the dealer has adapted a business practice that is considered by its peers as the preferred practice.

If I had to testify tomorrow, here is my list of industry standard as it applies to menus:

- The preferred process is a two-step process. The sale is closed, and the first step in the menu process is to generate the first page of the two-page documentation, or a Presentation Page;
- The F&I Manager is trained to memorialize the agreed upon sales terms with a statement like "These are the terms under which you've agreed to take delivery of the car today, with approved credit. The sale price is $20,000, with no down payment and a payment of $410 for 60 months at 4.9% APR. This may not be your best option, as I have some additional optional protections you may want to consider...";
- The base payment on the Presentation Page is then initialed by the customer. This affirms that the customer knew what she could take delivery of the vehicle for with approved credit, making every product purchased optional;
- The F&I products' features and benefits are listed on the Presentation Page;

- The second page is the Accept Declination page and it has two columns. One column is the list of products the customer accepted. The second column is the list of products the customer declined;
- The products selected on the Accept Declination page have a price for the product. That price matches all the other documents in the Paper and Digital Trail. Using the monthly effect of accepted products potentially breaks the Paper and Digital Trail because the monthly amount includes interest. Multiplying the monthly amount by the term does not match the product's price on any other document;
- The base and final payments are on the Accept Declination, confirming the payment walk; and
- Disclosures regarding products being optional, can be purchased separately, not required to obtain financing, and does not affect interest rate.

Risks of a Manual Menu

I've seen paper menu completed with enough different colored Sharpies to challenge a color wheel. Invariably, a paper menu completed with Sharpies will have many potential issues that put a dealer at risk of failing to meet the industry standard, bordering on potentially deceptive practices.

The manual menu process is a one-page process

It simply takes longer to handwrite all the terms of the sale, the base payment information, and the product prices on a paper menu that it takes to load the information into a web-based e-menu. This is the primary reason many practitioners of the manual menu only bother to complete the Presentation Page, using the color Sharpie of choice. The Accept Declination page is never contemplated, and likely not even available to complete. Instead, the manager simply pulls out the next color Sharpie to distinguish the first pass from the next pass and hopes it will be a transparent disclosure. Oh, how wrong that thinking is.

The sale is not always memorialized

Because it takes more time to handwrite the terms of the sale, the terms of the sale are sometimes not handwritten on the paper menu. By omitting the terms of the sale, one of the critical components of documenting compliance is lost and the Paper and Digital Trail takes a hit.

The base payment information is missing, incomplete, or packed

The manager must glean the base payment information (term, APR, and payment) from the DMS and transfer it to the manual menu with the trusted Sharpie. This additional step can mean that the manager neglects to disclose the information, only discloses the base payment and not the term or APR, or decides to add some leg to the payment to facilitate the sale of F&I products. "Look Ms. Customer, you can add the Warranty [sic], Gap, and Maintenance for only $10 more! Ain't I wonderful!!!" Obviously, none of these scenarios are protecting the dealership.

The APR is misstated

One of the Paper and Digital Trail requirements is that the APR matches from the menu to the Retail Installment Sales Contract. When the APR is misstated on the menu, it breaks the Paper and Digital Trail.

The base payment does not compute

Handwriting the base payment can lead to a misstatement of the base payment. When the rest of the sales information is used to calculate the base payment, it does not compute to the stated base payment. This could be considered a deceptive practice because of providing misleading information to the consumer.

The product prices are not disclosed

The Paper and Digital Trail requires that the price of products the customer selects is disclosed on at least three, and preferably four, documents the customer signs. The menu is one of these critical documents. Failing to disclose the prices of selected products breaks a portion of the Paper and Digital Trail the dealer is relying on to document compliance.

There is evidence of trading rate for product

Trading rate for product is a potentially deceptive practice. The Sherman Anti-Trust Act has a provision that a business cannot tie the price of one product contingent on the purchase of a second product. When the handwritten base APR is higher than the final APR, and the new base payment at the lower APR is not disclosed, the dark side can claim that the manager traded rate for product.

There is evidence of product stuffing

Let's assume that the manager properly memorialized the sale terms, accurately handwrote the base payment terms, correctly disclosed the final payment terms, and legibly wrote the prices of the products the customer selected in the ad-hoc column. The customer signs the menu and all is good, right? This still leaves open the possibility that the manager could later add another product to the ad-hoc column that the customer has no knowledge of. The manager just stuffed a product sale without the customer's knowledge.

It is not clears what the customer agreed to

Some managers ardently have circles, x-outs, and arrows in three different colors and believe the document demonstrates a clear and conspicuous decision on the customer's part to the purchase of F&I products. Nothing is further from the truth on some of the manual menus I see in red, blue, green, and black sharpies with three arrows, five circles, and two x-outs.

Some people simply have bad handwriting

Some humans simply have poor handwriting skills. Just as illegible as my two-year old grandson's writings. A manager who cannot write legibly has a rough time creating a manual menu that clearly shows the customer's acknowledgement of F&I purchases.

It breaks the important Paper and Digital Trail

Read the chapter titled The Paper and Digital Trail for a refresher on the importance of the Paper and Digital Trail in the defense of Dark Side claims against the dealer. A manual menu usually weakens the support of a dealer's potential defense if it is not properly completed and executed. It is a common trait of paper menus that they are not always properly completed and executed.

Most manual menu copies in manager's desk drawers really should be given to the local day care for coloring paper. There is more value to them at the day care.

Kinks Will Be Kinks

An e-Dealership uses an e-Menu in the F&I process to document customer decisions and sell products. Just like a e-Desking software, the kinks can still manipulate an e-Menu, either through the set up or other nefarious methods.

For example, one e-Menu provider uses a kiosk type set up to share the menu story. In one of my visits, I discovered that an F&I Manager (who I documented in the file review process was a bad apple) had a sticky note on the screen of his kiosk. The note said, "Call your wife" and had an illegible signature.

Turns out the guy wasn't married. Turns out the sticky note was strategically placed on the screen where the base payment disclosure sits. Turns out he was spinning a lot of deals without properly disclosing the base payment.

Kinks will be kinks.

Another risk to be wary of is the menu setup. Some systems permit a user an unlimited number of days to first payment. This will pack the base payment.

Other systems have multiple Accept Declination templates. Some of these templates do not provide all the industry standard information, such as suppressing the final agreed upon payment, or disclosing prices for selected products as the daily amount. These systems will allow a user to choose which Accept Declination to print. Turn off those options so that a user does not accidently print the wrong version.

Even with these potential risks, using an e-Menu is a superior approach to using a paper menu with a Sharpie.

The e-Menu

A fully compliant e-Menu will be created and signed using a two-page process. It begins with the Presentation Page and finishes with an Accept Declination Page.

An e-Menu is more efficient than a manual menu. The sales data can be pulled from the DMS. The base payment calculation is transferred to the Presentation Page correctly. The product prices are resident in tables so the correct price for the different terms or coverages are correct. The dealer's maximum pricing guidelines can also be set up in tables.

With an e-Menu, the Accept Declination Page becomes a more acceptable document for F&I Managers, who no longer must toil with Sharpies.

The Presentation Page will have all the industry standard disclosures. Some dealers will disclose the full price of the products on the Presentation Page, other dealers will suppress the full price of the products on the Presentation Page so that the customer will focus on the benefits story, not the cost story. Either approach is fine, just be sure to apply your choice consistently.

The customer should initial the base payment on the Presentation Page to demonstrate he knew what he could take delivery of the vehicle for without the purchase of products.

The Accept Declination Page is printed after the customer has made an informed choice. The products selected will be in one column, and the price of these products must be disclosed as the total premium, not the daily or monthly effect. The other column will list the products the customer declined during the presentation phase, and the prices can be listed as the monthly or daily amount. This option gives the manager one last shot at selling a product.

"For $8.42 a month, doesn't GAP really make sense in your situation?" If the customer agrees to purchase GAP on the second pass, print a new Accept Declination Page and include GAP as a purchased product with the full premium disclosed.

The final payment, term, and APR are also disclosed on the Accept Declination Page and the customer signs this document. The products selected, the prices for the products, and the final term, APR, and payment match the rest of the documents in the Paper and Digital Trail.

Properly executed…the e-Menu is a critical component of the Paper and Digital Trail many dealers rely upon in their compliance efforts.

CHAPTER 11

e-Contracting – Truth-in-Lending and Consumer Leasing Acts

KPOI FM was my radio station of choice in high school. My transistor and car radios never varied from 97.5 on the FM dial. I listened to KPOI FM driving to school, to the gym, to the beach, to the pool, at the beach, at the pool. At least until I finally installed an 8-Track player in the car.

I had images in my mind of my favorite disc jockeys spinning the tunes. The long-haired hippy DJ wore a set of headphones, sitting at a table with two turntables. To his left were the stack of albums and singles he intended to play that day. To his right, a beverage of choice or a bong or both. The Iron Butterfly album was set aside in its own special place so the 17-minute version of *Inna Godda Da Vida* hit the turntable when the bathroom or bong beaconed.

Sometimes the hiss and crackle from the scratches in the album came through loud and clear on the radio. Start the song before the track break on the album with the turntable needle and you listened to the finale from the last song.

Spinning records for a living.

Dr. Johnny Fever later confirmed this image on *WKRP in Cincinnati*, a classic television show from the late seventies and early eighties. Dr. Johnny was a crazy, has-been hippy with a fried brain. On the show, he sat at a table, spinning records. Two turntables. Headphones. Pots of Coffee. Long songs so he could take breaks or naps or whatever.

Spinning records for a living.

F&I Managers Spin Deals

F&I Managers spend their time spinning deals, not records, for a living. Even today, many F&I Managers are loading a paper RISC or Lease Agreement into a dot matrix printer, spinning the platen until the paper is set just right, and hitting the GO button. The printers that print correctly require little or no attention. The printers that slip or are set to the wrong speed or are not programmed to print correctly require that the F&I Manager watch and adjust the platen to print right. And the customer is watching and wondering…"WTF".

This is the analog approach and is fraught with potential issues and risks for dealers. These risks emanate from two Federal disclosure statutes: Truth-in-Lending Act (TILA) and Consumer Leasing Act (CLA). These Acts are strictly disclosure statutes. Some states have mini TILA and CLA statutes as well.

For example, TILA does not set a maximum allowable Annual Percentage Rate (APR), it simply requires the proper calculation and disclosure of an APR.

For example, the CLA does not mandate how rebates, positive trade equity, dealer non-cash credits, and customer cash are allocated, but simply how that allocation must be disclosed on the lease agreement.

Dealer Risks

I just left the dentist office. No Novocain this time, just a cleaning. While making my next appointment, the young lady behind the desk informed me with a somber face and sad voice that the office no longer sent out reminder postcards. She promised to call me before my next cleaning.

I proudly pulled my smart phone out of my pocket and gleefully informed her that I didn't need a stinking postcard, as I was no longer an analog guy in a digital world.

Another discussion I have too frequently is with Dealers Principals, Controllers, F&I Managers, or Sales Managers. Some are still operating under some old school misconceptions about contracts, still holding to a decades old view of proper processes. Analog folks in a digital world. Thankfully, no mullets were noticed in any of these discussions.

Some of the TILA and CLA misconceptions some Dealers and F&I Managers face include contracts printing offline, backdating contracts, backup contracts, prior loan or lease balance, and reprinting enrollment forms.

Contracts Off-Line

Misconception – It doesn't matter that the print doesn't line up on the contract; the customer knows what I meant.

An East Coast dealer can certainly clear up this misconception after it lost a TILA class action lawsuit because the first payment due date was obscured.

In 2012, US District Judge Warren Edington ruled that this East Coast dealer violated the federal Truth-in-Lending Act because the first payment due date printed on the pre-printed Retail Installment Sales Contract was obscured by the pre-printed language on the form. The finance source was a co-defendant as it funded the contracts.

Wrote the judge: *"The payment due date is not clear or conspicuous on any of the 104 contracts. The printed due dates range from indistinct to indiscernible, but an average, reasonable person could not find any of the disclosures to be clear and conspicuous."*

The plaintiffs claimed emotional distress because the payment due date printed from the Dealer Management System was programmed to print in an area on the contract where there was pre-printed language, thereby obscuring the due date.

Six figures and six years later, finance sources around the country are kicking contracts where the TILA disclosures are off-line and some dealers experienced higher contracts-in-transit, recontracting issues, some customer cancellations, and CSI issues. Of course, these contracts were the ones printed on the dot matrix printer (the analog approach) instead of e-contracted (the digital way).

If you decide to remain analog instead of digitally moving into e-contracting, you should periodically review the output from your DMS to ensure that all information is printing in the proper space on the proper form.

Or you can morph into e-Contracting and the alignment issue magically disappears. And your CITs will probably improve.

Backdating Contracts

Misconception – I must backdate the contract because…

Dealers have lost TILA violation cases from Virginia to California because the date of the contract is not the date it was signed. The theory successfully used by dark side attorneys is that dating a contract prior to its actual execution date charges interest during a period when there is not a consummated contract in place. Rolling the finance charge charged forward during this time and recalculating the APR creates a situation where the APR is not properly disclosed on the contract.

A 2002 lawsuit against a dealer in the East (*Rucker v. Sheehy Alexandria, Inc.*), followed by a landmark lawsuit against a West Coast dealer in 2007 affirmed that dating a retail contract on a date prior to the date of signing constitutes a TILA violation.

The 2002 lawsuit set forth the theory that a contract is consummated the date the consumer signs it. From the decision:

"According to Regulation Z, consummation occurs not when the consumer takes possession of the product, but at the 'time that a consumer becomes contractually obligated on a credit transaction.'"

Typically, with most recontracts, the second contract is signed on a date after the first contract, or date of delivery. The judge ruled that if a contract is dated prior to the date it is signed, the consumer is being charged finance charges when there was not a valid contract in place. Again, from the decision:

"Regulation Z does not permit calculation of the APR based on an interest accrual date which is earlier than the consummation date."

When you recalculate the APR using a shorter number of days to first payment, the APR disclosure is incorrect. If the variance is greater than .125%, the APR is not disclosed correctly as required by TILA and there is a technical TILA violation.

Simply put, there is not a valid reason to date a retail contract any other date than the date it is signed. There are four prevalent situations dealers use as excuses for backdating a contract. The 2007 California case identified some of these causes for recontracting, and none of them were accepted as an excusable reason to back date the Retail Installment Sales Contract. The four primary causes are:

Recontract

The transaction cannot be funded as spot delivered. When the customer comes back in to recontract, the F&I Manager did not update the DMS to reflect the current date and used the date of delivery on the second contract, not the date the customer signed the new RISC. In some states, contracts can only be rewritten if there was an error or omission on the first contract, not a credit decision issue. The requirement to properly date these contracts the date of signing still applies.

If a generation is considered every twenty years, it was the previous generation of Manufacturer's incentive auditors who would hit the dealer with a chargeback if the RISC was not dated within the incentive period, even on recontracts. This forced dealers to backdate the contract.

After the Rucker decision, the manufacturers have slowly come to the realization that the RISC is not the best source document to confirm the date of sale. When a dealer has properly recontracted the original deal, has an acknowledgement of rewrite, and voided docs from the previous transaction in file, the auditor now reviews other documents to confirm the date of sale.

Incentives

The customer agrees to purchase a vehicle after an incentive period expired and the Sales or F&I Manager agree to backdate the contract into the incentive qualifying period. This scenario carries the double sword of potentially putting the transaction in the scope of the manufacturer's incentive auditor and could create a chargeback.

Used Vehicle Value

The customer agrees to purchase a used vehicle shortly after the book value changed and the transaction bumps up against the approved loan to value ratio. In addition to the potential TILA violation, backdating this contract into a prior month could also be viewed as bank fraud by the lender.

Borrowed Vehicle

Infrequently, the dealer puts the customer out on a Borrowed Vehicle Agreement (BVA) and submits the credit application for approval instead of spot delivering the vehicle. Upon approval the customer returns to sign the paperwork, but the F&I Manager did not change the date of the deal in the Dealership Management System (DMS).

Any excuse for backdating a deal is inexcusable. Your Dealer Law must be that every RISC must be dated the date it is signed.

Other Industry Misconceptions

I field other questions, comments, and misconceptions in recap meetings and phone calls.

Misconception – There is no need to waste time to reprint the [insert F&I product name here] enrollment form.

F&I Managers make money selling products, not redoing paperwork. Unfortunately, recontracting deals means redoing paperwork. The recontracted deal must be thought of as a new transaction, because the first one is effectively voided (again, see The Paper and Digital Trail). The product enrollment form is effectively an addendum to the contract and it must be dated the same date as the contract.

Additionally, there are some finance sources that require that the date on the enrollment form matches the date of the contract. Assuming that the retail recontract is properly dated, that means the enrollment form must be reprinted, redated, and resigned.

Question – Why can't I do a backup contract?

I know this comes as a huge shock, but sometimes customers expect to take delivery of a vehicle today and bring you the $10,000 down payment next week.

Some dealers try to argue that they should be able to have the customer sign two contracts, one with the $10,000 down payment, one without the down payment. These dealers view this as an easier and effective way to handle the transaction whether the customer comes back with the down payment or not.

From a TILA perspective, if the second contract is the one cashed after the customer pays the $10,000 down payment, it is likely dated a previous date, resulting in the potential TILA violation previously discussed.

The dark side views a backup contract as a potentially deceptive and inexcusable practice since the dealer is effectively holding two contracts for the purchase of one vehicle. Again, any excuse is inexcusable.

Your policy should be to sign the customer to a contract without the down payment and offer to hold the contract for an acceptable period of days. This provides the motivation to the customer to bring the down payment in, at which point you will recontract the deal (using the current date). If the customer fails to show, you still have a contract you can present to a finance source for funding.

Leasing is Picking Up – What About Disclosures?

Leasing is the industry's roller coaster. It rattles around the bottom of the coaster after Risk Managers pull back on leasing because of residual losses. It starts ascending toward the crest again as Marketing Managers and manufacturers with short memories begin aggressively leasing to sell vehicles.

Leasing penetration as a percent of new vehicle sales bottomed out at around 16 percent in 2009 after enjoying a few years above 20 percent. In 2017, leasing accounted for roughly 30 percent of new vehicle sales, depending on which survey you rely upon. Many observers agree that leasing one-third of new vehicle sales is likely the new normal.

With this increase in leasing penetration, the plaintiffs' bar is interested in understanding the basics of leasing. After all, the logic goes, if dealers make TILA disclosure mistakes worthy of class action litigation because they can't always program the DMS correctly, can CLA disclosure mistakes be as prevalent?

A little primer on some common leasing disclosure issues is in order. The two greatest improvement opportunities on a lease agreement are the Itemization of Gross Capitalized Cost and the Amount Due at Signing sections.

Itemization of Gross Capitalized Cost (IGCC)

This section of the lease agreement discloses how the transaction builds from the Agreed Upon Price to the Gross Capitalized Cost. Certain items that can be included in the Gross Capitalized Cost include the lessor's acquisition fee, the dealer's doc fee, F&I products, prior credit or lease balance, taxes, and fees. The Agreed Upon Price must tie to the sale price the customer agreed to in the sales process.

Amount Due at Signing (Lease Starts)

This section lists the amounts that the customer must pay to start the lease. It includes such items as the capitalized cost reduction, first payment, security deposit, lessor's acquisition fee, dealer's doc fee, and upfront fees or taxes. These are paid by a combination of positive trade equity, manufacturer rebate, Dealer non-cash credits, and customer cash. The allocation of the of these contributions to lease starts are disclosed on the lease agreement.

Potential Disclosure Issues

Prior loan or lease balance is another way of saying negative equity. Just like on a retail deal, the lease disclosure statutes require the proper disclosure of any prior loan or lease balance included in the transaction.

The prior loan (negative equity from a retail trade) or lease (remaining lease payment, excess mileage, or excess wear and tear amounts to close the prior lease) balance cannot be added to the Agreed Upon Selling Price in the IGCC. Instead it is to be an itemized disclosure in the IGCC and labeled correctly. The proper disclosure of prior loan or lease balance does not affect the Gross Capitalized Cost or the customer's payment amount.

Some dealers make the mistake of including either negative equity or the last few lease payments in the Agreed Upon Selling Price.

The IGCC is an optional disclosure to be contained within the lease agreement. If the lessor opts to omit the disclosure from the lease agreement, it must include an option for the consumer to request a separate IGCC. Some F&I Managers are unaware of this requirement and admit they do not have the forms available to provide it to the customer if asked. If the lease agreement you use has this checkbox for the consumer to request the IGCC disclosure, make sure you have the forms to provide the disclosure and your DMS is programmed to print it correctly.

The lease starts section itemizes what the customer must pay to start the lease and how that amount is paid. The customer can settle up the lease starts with positive trade equity, manufacturer rebate, dealer non-cash credit, or customer cash.

A non-cash credit occurs when a dealer agrees to absorb a portion of or the entire lease starts. This can typically happen with a sign and drive lease, where the customer does not pay the first payment.

It is a common miscue to use cash collected as the plug number in setting up the deal and disclosing that the customer paid cash for the amount of the non-cash credit. Essentially, the amount disclosed as cash collected in the lease starts section must be supported with a receipt in the file. The amount absorbed by the dealer must be disclosed in the Rebate or Non-Cash Credit Line.

The third recurring issue with leasing is not with the lease agreement itself, but rather the lack of an Order for Leased Vehicle Agreement. Dealers outside of California generally have a Buyer's Order executed during the retail process. This Buyer's Order contains many reps and warranties and possible state required disclosures that are not necessarily contained within the Retail Installment Sales Contract. Many times, an Arbitration provision is contained within and agreed to on a Buyer's Order.

Some dealers continue to either try to fit a lease transaction on a Buyer's Order or they do not have any Order executed. Based on the 30 percent leasing penetration, this means that a dealer may not have the protection outlined in a Buyer's Order in nearly one-third of all new vehicle sales. Reynolds and Reynolds' has *LAW*® branded Lease Orders available in most states.

These three disclosure issues are as easily resolved as TILA disclosure issues on retail transactions. Just takes a little time and programming.

The e-Contracting Solution

e-Contracting eases the pain and angst of technical disclosure violations, as well as drives the additional benefit of improving contract-in-transit processes.

The two major advantages are numerical accuracy and no misplaced printing entries as with a dot matrix printed contract. You do need to get the consumer's prior consent under the ESIGN Act to do business electronically. In a single document rule state, these consents can be on contracts, but they should be obtained separately in advance, perhaps on a credit app form or a stand-alone document.

Customer copies can either be neatly and professionally printed by laser jet printer or saved to a flash drive and handed to the customer.

The e-Contract process won't let a practioner move forward unless disclosures are right, virtually eliminating potential TILA violations.

An e-Contract is dated the date it is executed, including recontracts. On a retail transaction, this eliminates a specific potential TILA violation of a misstated APR because the contract is dated a date prior to its execution. On a lease transaction, this updating can be problematic as the lessor usually will require that the lease be dated the date of vehicle delivery. This requirement is usually because the lessee is paying the first payment at delivery and because as residuals change, the entire lease transaction changes.

CHAPTER 12

Safeguards Through e-Storage

"Do unto others as you would have them do unto you."
- *Mt. 7:12 (The Golden Rule)*

The Safeguards Rule can be summed up by the Golden Rule. Treat your customer's non-personal, public information (NPI) as you would want your NPI to be treated where you bought or leased your car. The Safeguards Rule arose from the Gramm Leach Bliley Act in 2003. It is one of a few Federal Rules imposed on automotive retailers in the Federales' noble efforts to stem the tide of identity theft.

This rule requires auto dealers and other industries to establish, implement, and monitor a program to safeguards their customers' NPI from the swarm of identity thieves and rings.

The Safeguards Rule establishes five elements to a satisfactory information security program:

1. Designate a Program Coordinator (a.k.a. Compliance Officer);

2. Conduct a risk assessment;
3. Design and implement safeguards to control the risks you identify;
4. Oversee your service providers; and
5. Periodically audit and reevaluate your program.

Dealers must not only fulfill the five elements, they must also document their efforts in writing.

Designate a Compliance Officer

The Compliance Officer is responsible for directing the information security program and ensuring compliance with the provisions of the Safeguards Rule. The Compliance Officer must be an employee, who can then delegate any or all the remaining four components.

Conduct a Risk Assessment

The Rule requires dealers to identify reasonably foreseeable risks to the security, confidentiality, and integrity of customer information that could result in the unauthorized disclosure or other compromise of such information.

Design and Implement Safeguards

The Rule requires three specific types of safeguards to be put in place: administrative, technical, and physical.

- **Administrative safeguards** – would include, at a minimum, a dealership information security policy and employee training.
- **Technical safeguards** – while not specifically defined in the Rule, will most likely center on the dealership's computer network, and should include a vulnerability assessment which is a process that defines, identifies, and classifies the security holes in a computer, network, or communications infrastructure.
- **Physical safeguards** – primarily address threats to tangible embodiments of customer information.

Oversee Your Service Providers

The Rule requires dealers to oversee their service providers, i.e., those persons or entities that receive, maintain, process, or otherwise are permitted access to customer information through their provision of services directly to a dealer. Dealers oversee service providers by:

- Taking reasonable steps to select and retain service providers that can maintain appropriate safeguards for the customer information at issue;
- Requiring your service providers by contract to implement and maintain such safeguards; and
- Periodically review and audit service providers' compliance with the Safeguards standards they have established, and you have approved. This can consist of a review of their audit of their Safeguards program, preferably by an outside auditing firm.

Periodically Audit and Evaluate Your Program

Although the Rule requires periodic audits and evaluation of a dealer's security program, it does not suggest how often this must be done. Given the level of employee turnover in the automotive industry, a quarterly audit seems prudent, though a less frequent interval might be appropriate.

Often Overlooked Technical Risks

Many managers and compliance officers do an outstanding job of managing the paper risks in a Safeguards program. Double locking approaches to paper files, locked doors in offices that contain NPI, fax machines out of the public's view, etc. The sometimes overlooked risks are technical ones, and a lot of people assume that the dealership's IT Department is handling the risks. It is worth reviewing these potential risks. Some of these risks include keeping software and hardware up to date, establishing a security incident response team, doing periodic table top testing, doing annual vulnerability assessment tests, limiting employee permissions to customer data to only those people who need it to do their jobs, and disabling the ability to download data to external devices (with the possible exception of downloading customer copies during e-Contracting). You may also want to address the increasing phenomenon of BYOD (bring your own device) in which dealers let employees use their personal smart phones, tablets, and PCs to access dealer systems.

Analog Approach

I do not know of a dealer who was scanning deals or leveraging digital deal jackets when the Safeguards Rule became the law of the land. This means that every dealer started its Safeguards program using an analog approach. This approach included ensuring all offices where paper files could be stored were locked at night. Most dealers established a double lock system, in other words, a thief would have to get through two locks to steal a customer's file. The F&I Manager's office was to be locked and any files within the office were to be in a locked drawer. The Accounting office was to be locked, and all files within the Accounting Office were in locked filing cabinets.

The thefts and breaches were sometimes at night, by a cleaning crew who had keys. Other times, the theft happened with a thief meandering past an unoccupied, unlocked office close to the side exit and walked away with an armful of folders. Still other times, it occurred on a busy Saturday with the identity thief grabbing files left out in the open or in copier bins or fax receptacles.

Digital Solutions

Moving from paper deal jackets to digital deal jackets can be a more cost-efficient approach to storage. When you add the additional benefit of potentially implementing a better safeguarding approach to document storage, it seems to favor digital over analog. Some of a dealer's digital or scanning options include Reynolds & Reynolds, CDK, DSGSS, and other independent scanning companies.

Reynolds & Reynolds

An electronic deal jacket can be created in Reynolds & Reynolds starting with the sales process. Using its proprietary DocuPAD system, the F&I Manager is able to electronically execute or scan all of the documents created in the sales process into the DocuPAD Electronic Deal Jacket. Throughout the sales process the F&I Manager and other dealer personal may contribute to the Electronic Deal Jacket by scanning ancillary documents directly into the Electronic Deal Jacket or electronically creating them from the DocuPAD system which adds them to the Electronic Deal Jacket automatically creating a complete record of the transaction. The DocuPAD system and Electronic Deal Jacket enables the option for the dealership to print the customer copies of electronically signed documents or to save them to a USB drive to give to the customer

CDK

In CDK, digital deal files are created either by an employee scanning paper documents or by leveraging its desking, menu, and e-contacting options. Customer copies can be either printed as paper copies or saved to a USB drive.

DealerSafeGuardsSolutionS (DSGSS)

DSGSS provides a software solution that digitizes the documents generated in the sales process, has the flexibility to scan paper documents, then push the digital deal file to either Reynolds & Reynolds or CDK.

Other Scanning Solutions

There are other scanning solutions available to dealers and may be worth vetting as part of a dealer's move to digital deal jackets. Some of the companies I have worked with in the past include PDM, OneView, and DocuPro.

Regardless of which approach you take, once you decide to push your deal files from analog to digital, the safeguarding of your customers' NPI will be enhanced.

CHAPTER 13

Red Flags and Identity Verification

The car I was fast approaching drifted into my lane then back into its lane. The driver then sped ahead before slowing down again. Next, the car was drifting toward the median until the warning bumps alerted the driver to move back into his lane. "I gotta get around this drunk driver!" I thought to myself while looking for an opening to pass.

Eventually my chance came to make my move. I glanced over to see what a drunken idiot looked like; I was more than surprised to see someone who was reading from his smart phone. He was texting, not drinking.

Welcome to the new normal.

The new normal is slamming dealerships as well. Identity thieves have ramped up their games. Those dealerships that don't react and counter these changes will likely be left behind to face significant, if not severe, financial ramifications.

Identity Thieves

The recent spate of non-public personal information breaches has heightened the risk of personal identity theft throughout the country. In addition to major retailers and one credit reporting agency, a few dealers with robust Red Flags programs and processes in place have also recently experienced incidents of identity theft.

One recent war story illustrates how sophisticated the thieves have become. An apparent theft ring broke through a triple lock system at a luxury dealership earlier in the year and stole between 2,000 to 3,000 customer files.

One of the customers whose file was stolen had purchased her car with a personal check, a copy of which was in the file.

The ring created an authentic looking driver's license with the thief's picture and the victim's information. It created a watermark check to make a down payment, using the victim's banking information. The thief had a replacement insurance card and the credit application information.

The ring hit on a hot Saturday afternoon. Traveling over 500 miles, across mountains and state borders, they successfully drove back home with two luxury vehicles from two different dealers. To date, one vehicle was recovered; the other one is likely on a slow boat to China or Russia.

In an associated case, the thief had a synthetic ID and successfully answered all the out of wallet questions. Synthetic identity theft happens when identity thieves create new identities using a combination of real and fabricated information. Typically, the thieves will use a real SSN and pair it with a name not associated with that number. The SSN is typically one that is not actively being used, such as children or the deceased.

A synthetic identity thief may have a thin but current credit file from which the out of wallet questions will be generated. You must dig a little deeper than OOW questions if you suspect or your identity verification report suggests a synthetic identity thief.

The thief was part of the ring who successfully stole vehicles at two other dealers. The third dealer it hit thwarted the identity theft. The thief had a synthetic ID and answered the out of wallet questions as well. But this dealer had a gut feeling and probed further, uncovering the deceit.

Another War Story

The driver's license from a neighboring state looked authentic. The check for the down payment had a valid routing and account number. There was not an alert or address discrepancy in the credit report. The signatures on the docs matched the signature on the driver's license.

As we reviewed the file, with full knowledge that it was an identity theft, a few red flags did start waving.

The police ran the driver's license. The number on the driver's license in the file was off by one digit. The number on the driver's license in the file belonged to an Asian lady, the thief was African American, and the victim was Caucasian.

Urban rumor has it that identity thieves do not put any money down. However, in this case, the identity thief had information about the victim's checking account and had created legitimate looking checks to make a twenty percent down payment.

The insurance card was from the victim's insurance company, and a call to the listed agent confirmed that the victim had coverage. However, the insurance card had a notation that it was a "Replacement Card".

In retrospect, the F&I Manager and the salesperson recalled that the thief was constantly taking phone calls on her cell phone and was very protective of anyone seeing the caller's identity. They now suspect that the thief's third base coach was calling with instructions.

This weekend sale occurred when the dealership was busy and many of the businesses needed to confirm transactional information were closed.

Identity Theft Commonalities

Red Flags is one of the processes that lends itself very nicely to the e-Dealership concept. Many dealers leverage the vendor through which they pull a credit report to also run an algorithm to vet for potential red flags of identity theft.

This electronic vetting may not always be good enough, as witnessed by the dealer who had a gut feeling and probed further. Also unfortunate is that some of the supposed out of wallet questions (OOW) generated by some vendors have their answers contained within the credit report and if the thief has enough information to create a synthetic ID, it also likely has a copy of the credit report.

There were several additional red flags to this dealer that do not show up in the vendor's red flag algorithm. Common to all three thefts, the thief:

- Was from out of the area;
- Had never done business with the dealership before;
- Was purchasing a high end, but rather common vehicle; and
- Did not blink at MSRP pricing or the purchase of all F&I products.

The dealer that successfully thwarted the theft was able to confirm the victim's height and weight, which did not match the thief in the showroom. A quick call to the local police department resulted in the quick arrest of the thief. Had the dealer relied solely on the cleared red flags report from the vendor and a glimpse at the driver's license, it too would have suffered a loss.

This dealer has a few other tips to help manually vet transactions for potential theft:

- Check the email address provided with online credit apps to see if it makes sense for the applicant. Carlygirl69@gmail.com doesn't seem to make sense for a 65-year-old male;
- Review the identification closely. On the photocopy of the ID, if the font for name and address is clear and sharp, yet the physical characteristics and photo are slightly fuzzy, this may mean the ID was altered;
- Review the Social Security Number closely to make sure it is not a Credit Profile Number (CPN), also known as a Credit Privacy Number or Credit Protection Number. Identity theft rings and some not so honorable credit repair agencies create and encourage the use

of CPNs in lieu of SSNs. The three credit reporting agencies claim to have algorithms to notify creditors if the SSN used to request a credit report is a CPN;

- Push the customer to reduce the term from 72 months to 48 months and drastically raising the payment. If the person readily agrees, it may be a red flag that she or he has no intention to repay and may well be a thief; and

- Ask additional out of wallet questions that are not generated by your vendor. For example, ask the thief what her sign is (based on her birthdate), or what state he obtained his social security number in (based on the social security numbering methodology), or describe their home (based on a Google Earth satellite search).

Another dealer's file had a driver's license with a picture of two people. It looked like a picture you would take at the carnival photo booth. Yet, the address was correct for the name of the citizen on the driver's license. The social security number provided matched the social security number in the credit bureau report. The Red Flags vendor's algorithm did not identify any red flags or alerts. It appears the dealership relied solely on the vendor's clearing report and delivered the car on a bogus identification card.

And, if you stop to think about it, at least four people vetted the driver's license and thought it was sufficient to verify an identity: the sales person, the sales manager, the F&I manager, and the contract clerk. With two heads, one male, one female on the driver's license.

Vetting the Identification Card

My son used to work part time at a bouncer at a popular bar near a large university. Too many underage college students tried to get past him and into the drinking pits using fake IDs. He shared this process he was trained on to vet the ID card.

Take the card, look at the picture and physical description, then look at the person, then look at the ID again. If they don't appear to match, start the questions.

First question, "Your middle initial is 'A'. Does that stand for Aaron?" The key to this question is that the driver's license shows a middle initial of "L", not "A". The real person will answer, "My middle name is Leon." and you should feel better. If the person says "No, my middle name is Andrew." then you have someone in front of you who does not know his name, and it could be because it is a victim of identity theft's name, and not his.

Another question to ask is "What's your sign?" This, of course, requires that you know the birthdates for each astrological sign. Most people know their sign, but a sloppy identity thief may not know the sign of the person whose identity she has stolen.

Credit Freezes

I expect that there will be a drastic rise in the number of Americans who place a freeze on their credit bureau reports. As retailers who deal with credit reports in the completion of a high percentage of sales transactions, you need to know how to deal with the credit freeze.

A credit freeze is a good, descriptive term. It literally means that once the consumer places a freeze on his or her credit report, potential viewers such as auto dealers and finance sources can only view the information on the report after the consumer unlocks, or thaws, the report. Consumers hold the key to thawing a credit freeze.

The consumer must activate a credit freeze with each of the three credit reporting agencies, Trans Union, Equifax, and Experian. Part of the process of creating the credit freeze is a password or key code to thaw the freeze. The credit freeze is only as good as the security of the password or key code.

Once you encounter a credit freeze, follow these best practices:

- Inform the consumer of the credit freeze and the need for both you and the finance sources to be able to view the report;

- The consumer must then contact each credit reporting agency and request a thaw;
- Do not allow the customer to request the thaw using the dealership computer. If the deal ends up as an identity theft because the thief knew the password or key code, the IP address for the request will come back to the dealership;
- After providing the personal password or key code, the consumer will be able to thaw the freeze for a period;
- Recommend that the thaw be placed for at least a week to provide adequate time for potential finance sources to access and view the report; then
- Proceed with the deal.

Dealers are required to react to new and emerging risks as part of their Safeguards' and Red Flags' programs.

Because of the facts identified in these cases, dealers are wise to update their programs to include a policy on sales to out of state customers not personally known to the dealership (See Out of Area Deliveries for detailed information). Some points to consider include:

- Validate the identification with the NADA titling manual;
- Verify a second piece of identification (a work ID, a credit card that has been used are a few examples);
- Ask and validate the out of wallet questions available through several sources;
- Try to confirm the IP address for the online credit application is consistent with the customer's address;
- Consider obtaining thumbprints and videotaping F&I transactions;
- Call to confirm insurance coverage instead of relying on an insurance card; and
- Determine why the customer is in your dealership from out of the area. Have the sales person innocently ask the question and record

the answer. Then when F&I innocently asks the question an hour or more later, confirm the story stays the same.

REAL ID arrived!

Air travel is a great opportunity to spend a little time putting thoughts to words to books. The inspiration for this plane-written chapter was a sign in the airport security line:

"Effective January 22, 2018, each traveler must have a READ ID to pass through security", or something to that effect...

The date is right and the REAL ID requirement for air travel is real.

Evidently that obscure law that passed in 2005 with a three-presidential election future implementation date has snuck up on us like a Copperhead at night seeking a campfire.

So, what is the REAL ID Act?

Congress passed the REAL ID Act 2005. Its goal is to establish minimally acceptable security standards for state-issued driver's licenses and identification cards. It also prohibits federal agencies, like the local Air Force base or TSA from accepting licenses and identification cards for official purposes from those states whose ID vetting processes that do not meet these standards.

What are the deadlines for Compliance?

Two deadlines are looming:

- **January 28, 2018** – Anyone traveling through a TSA security checkpoint should use a driver's license or state issued ID card issued by states not in compliance with REAL ID standards. They can still use a valid passport to get through security.
- **October 1, 2020** – Anyone wanting to fly or enter a federal facility that requires identification must have a REAL ID compliant driver's license, state ID or passport. So, all those folks in Arizona with

driver's licenses that expire on their 65th birthday will have to renew early to obtain a REAL ID compliant driver's license.

Are there any states who don't comply with REAL ID?

The REAL ID Act is a mandate for Federal Agencies to confirm the identity of anyone wanting to enter or use its facilities. It is not a national identification law, which leaves state compliance as a voluntary decision.

Most states are either fully compliant or have been granted an extension to the January 2018 guideline. There are, however, states and U.S. territories who are still under review for an extension, leaving their citizens at risk of the January 2018 deadline. Some of these states may issue Enhanced Driver's Licenses which are an acceptable option.

What does it take to be compliant with REAL ID?

The state issuing the Driver's License or Identification Card must vet documentation the consumer provides to positively prove the following:

- A photo ID, or a non-photo ID that includes full legal name and birthdate;
- Documentation of birth date;
- Documentation of legal status and Social Security number; and
- Two documents showing name and principal residence address.

How does the READ ID Act affect dealers?

I renewed my driver's license shortly before sending this book to the printer. I ran into a bit of a snafu with my DMV Clerk. The last name on my birth certificate is one word "Vanover". My dad has always told us our last name is two words "Van Over" with the space and capital O. My current driver's license has it as two words, but the clerk was adamant that the driver's license had to match the date of birth documentation I provided to obtain the REAL ID. Then we looked at my passport. My last name is two words on that document. The clerk ended up using my passport for my date of birth documentation instead of my birth certificate, and my last name is two words on the driver's license.

I've learned of other issues that have surfaced because of the varying states complying with the REAL ID Act that potentially affect dealerships and more specifically, the dealership's Red Flags compliance requirements.

The first one, and more commonly seen, is when the Driver's License or ID card have a designation on it stating, "Not Valid for Federal Identification". At first blush, this certainly gives one pause about the validity of the identification and whether it can be accepted as identification to sell and finance a vehicle. As we have learned, the ID is likely valid (unless it is an obvious forgery) as identification to prove compliance with Red Flags, OFAC, Dealer-Lender Agreement, and any other requirement to positively identify your customer.

However, it is buyer beware for dealerships on a case by case basis. I recently saw a deal from a County Credit Union with a stip for US Driver's License: Applicants with "Federal Limits Apply" stamp are not eligible for CU membership. Watch out for those stips!

The second one, like in my instance, is a result of an individual who renewed his driver's license. After going by a surname all his life, and he was born around the time President Kennedy was assassinated, he produced his birth certificate document his birth date. It turns out his parents were not married at the time of his birth, and the surname on his birth certificate is different than the surname on his current driver's license, military ID, DD214 and Costco card. So, to be compliant with the READ ID ACT, his new Driver's License has a new surname. Talk about a conundrum!

In this case, the dealer thoroughly documented its file to demonstrate the steps it used to comply with Red Flags. These steps included:

- Short story in customer's handwriting outlining the history of his surname and change;
- Successful answering of OOW Questions;

- Retained copies of DD-214 and additional photo ID (not the Military ID);
- E-mail discussion with the finance source before the credit decision; and
- General Manager approval to deliver the vehicle.

Unfortunately, this has also prompted the dealer to contemplate yet another form to document these types of cases. Another form usually seems to be an unintended consequence of new laws and compliance with those laws.

In Addition to REAL ID

Permit me to be a little facetious…

You can't get on an airplane with an expired driver's license.

So, you can perhaps understand my disbelief when the Sales Manager insists that you don't need a driver's license to buy a car. So, the diatribe continues, why should the Office Manager stop a deal because it doesn't have a valid, unexpired ID?

Let me share a few war stories from dealers who chose to look the other way when the customer simply did not have a valid U.S. government issued ID. Or simply forgot to verify identity.

Michigan has a repeat offender law that disqualifies anyone convicted of multiple DUI's from registering a vehicle. A dealer across the state line sold a car to a Michigan resident, obtained a copy of an expired driver's license, and did not check the Michigan Secretary of State website to confirm that the customer was not a repeat offender, which she was. The dealer was not able to register the financed vehicle, thereby violating the dealer lender agreement and had to pay off the loan.

You can't rent a car with an expired driver's license.

Good luck getting into a bar with an expired driver's license.

A dealer in the Midwest accepted a Mexican Matricula card on a Hispanic customer in lieu of a valid U.S. government issued ID on a financed deal. The finance source ultimately repossessed the vehicle and the recovery department discovered that the customer had purchased his social security number in 2005. Now the dealer is being asked to repurchase the loan.

My guess is that a police officer would write you a ticket if you were pulled over and presented an expired driver's license.

There are many reasons why someone *does not* have a current driver's license and most of them are bad:

- Honest oversight;
- Lazy;
- Couldn't pass the written or driving test on renewal;
- Has a current driver's license from another state;
- Identity theft;
- Not eligible for insurance; or
- Not eligible for other criminal reasons.

Just because some states do not require a current driver's license to register and title a vehicle, there are other, over-reaching requirements on car dealers that suggest you should have a legible, current form of U.S. government issued ID on every deal. The most common form of ID is a driver's license, but a state ID card, or Passport is also acceptable.

OFAC requires you to check its list of Specially Designated Nationals (SDN) a.k.a. suspected terrorists, drug dealers, and money launderers to ensure your customer is not on the list.

The Red Flags Rule requires you to confirm you are not selling a vehicle to an identity thief. Your Red Flags policy likely or should require a current, legible government issued ID on every financed deal.

On financed deals, even though the finance source may not require a form of ID to fund the deal, it usually reserves the right under your dealer-lender agreement to check your files at any time to confirm that you verified identity.

Therefore, you should have a legible, current government issued ID in every deal.

Finance Sources

Many of the sub-prime finance sources are asking for copies of down payment receipts on deals that have defaulted, sometimes up to four years after the vehicle purchase. In some cases, these same finance sources are requesting a contract buy back by claiming that the stips provided by the dealer were not legitimate or potentially manufactured.

They are looking for potential violations of the Dealer-Lender agreement which would require the dealer to buy the deal back. Put another way, they are looking to shift the loss from them to you.

As a best practice response to these inquiries from finance sources, many dealers implemented a process for the collection and submission of stips: Get 'em, Vet 'em, Copy 'em, and Submit 'em.

The new normal is time consuming and requires a change to existing processes. The alternative, though, is nasty and wallet thinning.

More dealers today are taking the same approach to documenting the clearing of Red Flags. Some managers have started the practice of manually overriding a potential red flag so that the summary report available in all vendor systems shows an "All Clear". If a deal has an address discrepancy, simply override the red flag. Social Security Number discrepancy? Override it. Fraud alert, credit freeze? Override them all!

This practice of managing the report instead of managing the transaction is leaving some dealers at risk of delivering a vehicle to an identity thief. When the victim raises a concern or worse yet, a regulator starts asking questions, the dealer's file shows that the manager was alerted to a potential red flag and took a laissez faire approach to vetting the discrepancy or alert.

Apart from the risk of selling to an identity thief, dealers are starting to run into other ancillary issues, even if the customer is truly the customer.

The finance sources that we sell contract to are also required to maintain a red flags program and some are running red flags checks that are a little more sophisticated than the dealer's program does. These finance sources are stipping dealers for documentation to clear the red flags in their files, such as proof of roof (POR) or copies of Social Security cards.

I recently reviewed a transaction where the dealer's red flag software identified an address discrepancy. The customer listed three months at the residence on her credit application. The dealership manager clicked the "All Clear" button so that the report shows the ID Verification was completed.

The problems started when the finance source stipped the deal for POR, because the finance source had to clear the same discrepancy. 20 days later, the customer finally showed up with acceptable POR and the deal was funded. But the deal continued to rise the CIT list in daily Save-A-Deal meetings instead of being funded within a few days.

Analog Approach to Red Flags Compliance

The Red Flags Rule does not require that a dealer utilize a digital solution to comply with its requirements. It simply states that the business' Identity Theft Prevention Program (ITPP) is reasonable for the size of the business. The FTC provided a list of suggested Red Flags to be checked on each transaction.

The dealer could establish an ITPP based strictly on an analog review of the credit bureau report, the identity provided, and the credit application information, further review of any additional potential red flags itemized in the ITPP and complete a manual report.

The credit bureau report will provide any potential discrepancies that must be addressed. For example, the dealership manager enters the customer's address and social security number into the query when requesting a credit bureau report. The credit bureau has an algorithm for providing potential Red Flags in its report that compares the input address and social security number to the same information within the customer's credit bureau file. If there is a difference between the two, the credit bureau reports a discrepancy between the two. It is then left to the dealer to reconcile the discrepancy.

One of the suggested red flags the FTC identified is an excessive number of new inquiries. The thought is that an identity thief may be on a shopping spree with the victim's identity. An analog approach to clearing red flags would then also require that the manager thoroughly review the inquiry section of the credit bureau report for excessive inquiries.

One approach to clearing a potential red flag is the use of OOW questions. The Feds intended for OOW questions to be questions that an identity thief would not necessarily have access to if the thief has the victim's driver's license, passport, and credit bureau report. A dealer implementing an analog solution to red flags will struggle developing four questions that are not part of the driver's license or credit bureau report. For example, "How much is your mortgage payment?" is part of the credit bureau report. "When is your birthday?" is on the driver's license. A good identity thief will know these answers. And good luck generating the second set of questions if the customer fails the first time around.

The dealership's ITPP should then require the manager to review the discrepancy and obtain enough information to confirm that the difference is legitimate, not due to an identity thief providing misleading information.

Sounds time-consuming and fraught with potential oversight or errors to me. Which is one of the many reasons that most dealers use a digital solution for red flags compliance.

Digital Solutions for Red Flags Compliance

Every software vendor who supplies dealers with credit bureau reports also provide a Red Flag software solution. They all have their nuances, and the summary reporting may vary, but each is an acceptable digital solution to help a dealer manager the transactions and process, not a report.

These vendors use algorithms which not only compares the dealer's input to the information in the credit bureau, but also pings against many other databases for information not contained in the credit bureau. I was once asked where I lived when I was in the fifth grade. Thankfully I remembered the answer. Thankfully I was consulting with the vendor and was able to ask how in the world the vendor knew my address while I was in elementary school. Keep in mind, my dad was in the Air Force and we moved every three or four years. It turns out that one of the databases this vendor pinged off is the list of subscribers to *Boy's Life* magazine and as a loyal Boy Scout in the fifth grade, I had a subscription. A dealer using an analog approach would never have such a question to include in its list of OOW questions.

Typical Red Flags Clearing Process

A Red Flags verification is run in the vendor's software when the credit bureau report is pulled. If the score returns as "Incomplete" or "Failed" or "Caution", the manager is to stop the transaction until the red flag identified in the report is vetted and documentation is obtained to properly clear the red flag.

Typical red flags that can appear on the credit report are:

- Address discrepancy;
- Social Security Number discrepancy;
- Vendor's software is unable to positively identify the customer;
- Fraud alert in credit report;
- Active duty alert in credit report; or
- Credit freeze on the credit report.

The manager is required to clear all of these red flags before proceeding with the transaction. The documentation used to clear the red flag must be retained. Simply hitting the update button without investigating the issue and documenting the results is not acceptable.

Acceptable Clearing Documentation

Some managers are under the mistaken impression that obtaining a clearing score by successfully answering the OOW questions is all that is needed to clear the red flags report.

This tool is a great tool for many of the red flags that can show in the red flags report, but does not adequately clear address discrepancies, social security number discrepancies, active duty alerts, or credit freezes. These specific red flags require other clearing documentation. One reason is that some of the OOW questions are from the credit bureau report and can be successfully answered by an identity thief. Another reason is that the finance source will likely stip for documentation to clear the red flag, and since the finance source will rarely call the customer to obtain answers to OOW questions, they rely on clearing documentation provided by the dealer.

Address Discrepancy

This Red Flag is a result of a difference between the address input to request the credit bureau report and the address the credit bureau report has on file. This is usually the result of either a) a typo when inputting the address; b) the customer recently moved, and the credit bureau address has not been updated; or c) the address provided by the customer is incorrect.

If the difference is a result of a typo, make sure the address on the documents is corrected and noted on the clearing media. If the red flag is because of (b) or (c), then obtain acceptable proof of residence, review it for correctness, make a copy, and attach it to the clearing media. Some of your finance sources will define acceptable proof of residence, such as utility bill (gas, electric, etc.), land line phone bill, cell phone bill (excluding a prepaid cell phone program), cable or internet bill, current paystub (must include company name, and name and address of customer), mortgage statement, bank statement (checking or savings), real estate/escrow tax till, or credit card statement. Vehicle registration, driver's license, or insurance card are not acceptable documents for proof of residence.

Social Security Number Discrepancy

This red flag is a result of a difference between the Social Security Number input to request the credit bureau report, or many other searches for the validity of the Social Security Number conducted against other databases, such as the Social Security Administration's Death Master File.

If the difference is a result of a typo, note it on the clearing media, print or scan, and retain a copy of the clearing media. All other differences must be cleared with documentation from the customer and include a copy of the Social Security Card or an award letter from the Social Security Administration. Vet the documentation for accuracy and validity, make a copy, attach the copy to the clearing media, and retain a copy in the file or digital deal jacket.

Fraud Alerts

A customer's consumer report may contain an initial or extended fraud alert. Both instances require additional diligence in the customer identity verification process.

An initial fraud alert stays on the consumer report for 90 days and indicates that the customer believes he or she may have been a victim of identity theft. Require additional photo identification and documentation (for example, utility bills, etc.) when verifying the customer's identity. If the consumer report indicates a specific means to be used to identify the customer (e.g. calling the customer at a specific phone number), use that means as well. Document the additional efforts to verify the customer's identity on the vendor's clearing media.

An extended fraud alert stays on the consumer report for seven years and indicates that the customer has notified the authorities that he or she has been a victim of identity theft. The consumer report will indicate a specific means to be used to identify the customer, and you must use this means. Also, use the additional verification methods you would use in the case of an initial fraud alert. Document the verification on the vendor's clearing media.

Identity Not Authenticated

This red flag occurs either because the vendor was not able to authenticate the identity through the databases it subjects the customer's information to. To clear this red flag, obtain a second piece of photo identification and ask the OOW questions available in the vendor's software. The customer must successfully answer the OOW questions to clear this Red Flag. The purpose of asking OOW questions is to affirm that the information gathered during the transaction belongs to the individual attempting to purchase the vehicle. Care must be taken not to feed the correct information to the individual(s) being questioned, but to set up a non-threatening scenario whereby only *someone with intimate knowledge* would know the correct answers.

Do not ask questions that pertain to items such as Driver's License Number, Vehicle Insurance Information, Credit Cards, and Social Security Number because this information could have been obtained by unlawfully using someone's wallet that was lost or stolen.

Active Duty Alerts

If the customer's consumer report contains an active duty alert, obtain a military ID from the customer as well as orders indicating where he or she is stationed and a Leave and Earnings Statement (LES).

You can make a copy of the orders and LES to attach to the clearing media. Retain a copy in the file. You cannot make a copy of the Military ID card.

In RouteOne, the clearing media is contained within the Credit Report/IDOne Manager page. Review the Red Flag issue and document the action taken to clear the Red Flag. Retain in the deal file or scan into DocuPAD Digital Deal Jacket.

In Dealertrack, the clearing media is the Customer Investigative Report (CIR). Review the Red Flag issue and document the action taken to clear the Red Flag. Print the CIR and attach any paper documents used to clear the Red Flag. Retain in the deal file or scan into your digital deal file

In 700 Credit, the clearing media can be accessed the Manual Override button found on the Red Flag Summary Screen. Once the clearing documentation information has been collected, the user selects the "Override Status / Add Notes" button and manually enters the steps taken to clear the red flag(s).

In CDK, the clearing media is an extension of the red flags report. Clearing action can be documented on the report, and the report can be printed with the clearing documentation attached, or both can be scanned into the Digital Deal Jacket.

Refreshing the Policies

Think of the differences between the 2003 model you sold years ago and the new model on your showroom today. The technological advances will blow you away.

These same types of technological advances are available to identity thieves. We must update our identity theft policies and procedures to account for these new threats.

Some dealers are also reporting that the newer Dealer-Lender Agreements contain stronger language regarding identity theft deals and that they become recourse, even if the dealer followed all the appropriate processes and protocols.

This brings to light some of the preventative measures dealers may want to implement to prevent becoming a victim.

- Require U.S. or state issued IDs (passport, driver's license, state ID). Do not accept a Mexican Matricula Card, employer ID, or school ID as the primary piece of identification;
- In states that permit it, verify every driver's license with the state's Division of Motor Vehicles;
- Compare the driver's license provided by out-of-state customers with the examples in the NADA Titling Guidebook or online via a Google search;
- Be wary of out-of-area buyers. The back story as to why she is in your dealership 400 miles from home must be plausible and could prompt some checking;
- Automatically run and require successful answers to OOW questions on out-of-state customers;

- Physically review a credit card in the customer's possession on out-of-state and questionable customers. Verify that the name is the same and that it has not been issued recently;
- Retain or have access to verification that the customer answered the OOW questions correctly, then shred the answers provided by the customer;
- Consider obtaining thumbprints on all customers not personally known to the owner or General Manager. Dealers who obtain thumbprints report occurrences of people conveniently finding excuses to leave when asked for thumbprints;
- Don't assume that multiple inquiries on the credit report are a result of the customer shopping. Instead, call the other dealer to confirm it did not sell the customer a vehicle;
- Review the provided email address. Beware of an email address that does not seem to match the customer's name. brutusbuckeye#1@email.com may not be a good email for someone wearing a Michigan sweatshirt;
- Take the task of verifying insurance seriously. Be wary of replacement insurance cards,
- Ensure that the information on any proof of address, proof of income, and insurance cards is accurate and consistent. One dealership biller noticed during her compliance checklist review of a deal file that the utility bill in the file to verify proof of address listed the customer and the customer's address at the top of the utility bill but had the F&I Manager's name and address in the detachable slip to accompany the payment. It seems the FI Manager saved her utility bill to a PDF file, then used the PDF Editor function to change her name and address to the customer's name and address. She did a half-butt job and is now looking for another job. And;
- Establish a Dealer Law that cell phones be silenced during the F&I close.

Identity theft is serious, the thieves are serious, the consequences are serious, and the harm to both the victim and the dealer are serious. You should take your responsibility serious as well. It's time to update.

CHAPTER 14

Out of Area Deliveries

When people get in trouble, it is not always because they are bad people. They could be good people who make bad decisions.

Here's a story of good people who made a series of bad decisions. A dealer recently reported an identity theft scenario.

The thief called from seven state lines away asking about a car he saw on the dealer's website. An eager Salesperson accepted the victim's credit application information by phone. Upon request, the thief faxed what appeared to be the victim's driver's license. The aggressive Sales Manager ran a credit report, penciled a deal for an "A" tier customer, to which the thief negotiated the down payment away.

True to the usual process, the F&I Manager submitted the deal to a finance source through one of the available aggregator systems and obtained a system approval. She then printed the paperwork and sent it to the "business address", which turned out to be a drop box. The thief signed the paperwork, sent it back, and called the sales person to arrange for the transportation of the car to the victim's address.

Roll forward a few days. The transport driver calls the thief on the thief's disposable cell phone to give him the ETA. About an hour before the car was due to arrive, the thief calls the driver and reports that he is still at the mall. He arranges to have the car dropped off outside of Sears.

Now, this dealer is a good person. His people are good people. They just made a series of bad decisions which could have prevented this from happening. Let's dissect.

The phone call – is something we strongly advise against. Accepting credit apps over the phone makes it too easy for identity thieves to pull one over on the dealership. If someone from out of the area wants to submit credit information, accept it through your website on a secure website. However, if you insist on accepting phone apps, develop a process, including a script, and ask out of wallet questions to help confirm the applicant's identity.

The driver's license – was a fake. A good one, but a fake. When the dealer eventually compared the faxed driver's license against a sample from the massive book in the Accounting Office which has samples from all 50 states and Puerto Rico, it was obvious the faxed version was a fake. The Governor's signature on the Driver's License was in an internet font. The Governor had moved on to greener pastures when the Driver's License was issued and was no longer in the Governor's Mansion.

The business address – was a short-term rental drop box mail facility. Red, Purple, Pink, and Mauve flags should have been waving throughout the dealership when the thief requested that the paperwork be sent to a different address than the home address. Further verification of the business address could have stopped this transaction from occurring.

The transport driver – did not follow his instructions to deliver the car to the home address. Instead, thinking he was providing superior customer service, he agreed to deliver the car to a parking lot. At a minimum, he should have called the dealership and advised them of the change in delivery request.

Even with the advantages and benefits of moving into the digital world, some risks have also amplified. Going digital also means clearing some roadblocks for identity thieves, potentially making it easier to steal a victim's identity and your inventory.

Out of Area Delivery Defined

An Out of Area Delivery is any transaction where the customer lives outside of a dealer's geographic footprint. Some identity theft cases involve customers who visited a dealership a few states away from the victim's residence with manufactured identity and stips. In other cases, the ID thief conducted the entire transaction by phone and internet and the vehicle was shipped.

Caution – Out of Area Deliveries

When you reverse engineer an identity theft case, you will likely find some signals (or red flags) which may have prevented the crime. Sometimes these signals are overlooked or ignored in the rush to seal the deal.

Obviously not every Out of Area Delivery is an identity theft, but some of the more blatant thefts end up violating one of these observations:

- The customer is not in the geographic footprint of the dealership;
- The dealer has never done business with the customer before;
- The customer accepts prices and options without debate;
- There is rarely a down payment or trade; and
- The customer never steps foot in the dealership.

Your sales and F&I processes should put a huge caution sign on any transaction that checks one or more of these signals and take the time to properly vet the customer against your Red Flags process.

Process – Out of Area Deliveries

The Out of Area Delivery process should be a separate and distinct part of your Sales and F&I Policy Manual.

Obtain and Vet the Credit Application

The credit application is one of the first signals of an Out of Area Delivery. When the customer's address is outside of the dealer's geographic footprint, immediately start the vetting process.

Why is the customer trying to purchase a vehicle from us? Especially salient if the vehicle is a model that you have a 100-day supply of.

Has the customer ever done business with us before? If so, pull up the information from prior deals from your CRM and see if it matches the information you are now being provided with.

Pull up a satellite image of the residence address. Be careful if you find a warehouse or a campground. Or if the shack in the image does not support a $5,000 a month mortgage as stated on the credit application.

Take a close look at the email address provided by the applicant. Does the email conflict with the other information available? For example, goofygirl@gmail.com may not be consistent with a 72-year-old man.

Conduct a social media search, including Facebook and LinkedIn. Compare information from those searches with the information on the credit application and the State ID or Driver's License. This is sometimes a great resource to compare photos between the two.

Vet the Identity Provided

You are familiar with the state generated identities from your state, and maybe even neighboring states. You may not be so familiar with a State ID or Driver's License from another region.

Use a search engine to view images of valid other state ID or Driver's Licenses. Another option is to review the ID against the images in the NADA License and Titling Guide.

Ask for another photo ID.

Confirm that the wear and tear on the ID is consistent with the age of the ID. If the ID was issued three years ago and appears brand new – watch out.

Confirm that the signing authority, sometimes the Governor, sometimes the person in charge of the DMV, was in office when the identity was issued.

Review the font on the state issued identity. The font style and size are usually consistent by state.

Complete the Red Flags Review

Most dealers today use an automated process to conduct the bulk of its red flags review. With authorization to pull a credit report in hand, run the red flags review and ensure there are no red flags noted. If there are any red flags, proceed with your clearing process and retain all documentation used to clear the red flags.

Use the available out of wallet questions as an added precaution, particularly if the customer is not and will not be in the dealership. Enhance your process by obtaining the answers via a Skype or Facetime session. Focus on the body language of the person on the other side of the call and compare that person to the picture on the provided identity.

Complete the Paperwork

For those customers who you have decided to ship the paperwork to, you should seriously consider using available services such as Maverick Signings or Superior Notary Service that will send a notary to the customer's residence to complete the signing of all paperwork.

Alternatively, send the paperwork to the address on the credit application with delivery signature required. Note every spot the customer is to sign and require the signatures be notarized. Also require the Notary to make a copy of the customer's identity and confirm the identity is consistent with the person signing the paperwork.

When the paperwork is received, confirm the Notary is legitimate.

Another option is to send the customer to an affiliated dealership to sign the paperwork if you have an affiliated dealership in the area.

Deliver the Vehicle

Many of the out of area deliveries that became identity theft cases have a common thread. The thief called the driver of the shipping company and had the delivery diverted to an alternative address.

Make certain to get it in writing that the shipping company is to contact you if such a request is made before continuing with the delivery.

Provided your manufacturer or finance source do not prohibit Out of Area Deliveries, they can be a lucrative approach to sell vehicles. It is also a lucrative method for identity thieves to steal your inventory and some unsuspecting citizen of his or her identity.

Don't be more anxious to sell the car than the thief who wants to steal it.

CHAPTER 15

OFAC

On the TV show *24,* Jack Bauer was a super terrorist defeater extraordinaire. One season, he was released from a foreign prison after spending a few birthdays and immediately returned to prime form in ferreting out and defeating terrorists. While we mere mortal viewers were encouraged to suspend reality to follow Jack's exploits and the plot (ever notice Jack's cell phone never dropped calls or ran out of juice) the moral of the story remains true.

American citizens must remain vigilant in our fight against terrorism.

The Office of Foreign Assets Control (OFAC) administers and enforces economic sanctions programs primarily against countries and groups of individuals, such as terrorists, money launderers, and narcotics traffickers, called Specially Designated Nationals, or SDNs. OFAC maintains and constantly updates an SDN list. Through OFAC, dealers and other Americans have been deputized into Jack's posse in the government's fight on the war on terrorism. Welcome to reality.

I have written a handful of articles over the years about a dealer's requirement to check its potential customers against the government's OFAC list of suspected terrorists, drug dealers, money launderers and those engaged in activities related to the proliferation of weapons of mass destruction. Some dealers respond with "When was the last time anybody had an actual OFAC hit?"

I normally respond that the chance is unlikely that someone on the list would be out buying a car, but the potential penalties of jail time, fines, and forfeiture of assets were too great to ignore. In 2008, however, there was news of an OFAC hit. Direct from the web on YahooSports.com. "As interest has grown in the NBA over signing 7-foot-2 Iranian Olympian Hamed Ehadadi, the league office has sent a letter to its 30 teams instructing that they are forbidden to even discuss a contract with Ehadadi, Yahoo! Sports has learned. In the letter, which was sent Friday, NBA legal counsel wrote: "It has come to our attention that representatives of Hamed Ehadadi, an Iranian basketball player, may be contacting NBA teams to discuss the possibility of signing Mr. Ehadadi to an NBA player contract. "We have been advised that a federal statue prohibits a person or organization in the United States from engaging in business dealings with Iranian nationals." The NBA is applying to the U.S. Office of Foreign Assets Control for a license that, "if granted," the league said, would allow teams to negotiate with the 23-year-old Ehadadi. Until then, no franchise is allowed to do so."

I know…it is not someone on the list buying a car, but the list is active, the risk still applies.

Been Around a Long Time

OFAC-type regulations have been around since prior to the War of 1812 and have morphed into today's OFAC. Prior to the War of 1812, The U.S. Treasury administered sanctions imposed against Great Britain for the harassment of American sailors. Fast forward to the Civil War (or as my dad calls it, the War Between the States), Congress approved a law which prohibited transactions with the Confederacy.

In 1940, the Office of Foreign Funds Control was established at the advent of World War II following the German invasion of Norway. A decade later, in December 1950, OFAC formally succeeded the Office of Foreign Funds Control when China entered the Korean War.

Our OFAC Obligation

From OFAC's website: "All U.S. persons must comply with OFAC regulations, including all U.S. citizens and permanent resident aliens regardless of where they are located, all persons and entities within the United States, all U.S. incorporated entities and their foreign branches. In the cases of certain programs, such as those regarding Cuba and North Korea, all foreign subsidiaries owned or controlled by U.S. companies also must comply." Still there?

Governmentese Translated

There is legalese, then there is governmentese. Simple translation of the OFAC requirement means that all US citizens, including automotive dealers, must check each customer against the OFAC list. You must check the OFAC list on all vehicle sales: credit, cash, lease, or wholesale. The requirement is straightforward. It says you must check OFAC for any person you do business with.

That does not mean only the parties on the contract. It also means anyone contributing financially to the deal, known in the business as third parties. If you accept a trade from the dad, and he is not on the contract, you need to run an OFAC on the dad. If the customer writes a check from his business account, you must check the business. If mom pays the down payment, and is not on the contract, check out mom.

As part of a dealer's Safeguards program, you should take this one step further and check all prospective employees against the OFAC list.

OFAC Availability

For those of you using an analog process, print the OFAC list from the government's website and manually search for the name or business for every party to every transaction. Then make a copy of the page where the person or business would be listed and retain in the file to prove you checked OFAC before selling the vehicle. You also need to print the new list every time the list is updated, which can be frequently. By the way, make sure you print all 1077 pages of three column listings. Every time the list is updated.

From a digital approach, the definitive place to check if your customer is on the OFAC list is the OFAC list. The OFAC website has a search functionality which facilitates the search. Save it to your desktop for future use.

Every software provider that resells credit bureau reports automatically run an OFAC check. Pull your bureau through RouteOne? An OFAC check is included. Use Dealertrack? OFAC is run there as well. Same with 700 Credit, CBC, ProMax, and any other provider of credit reports.

If you have a process where you do not pull a credit bureau report, you can check the OFAC website or other OFAC search software providers, such as Instant OFAC.

What if I Get a Hit?

As I mentioned, the OFAC list is periodically and frequently updated. I subscribe to the OFAC's e-mail notification service which alerts me when the list is updated. There have been weeks when I received three e-mails with updates.

The credit bureaus' OFAC search engine incorporates these frequent updates when they occur. If you receive a potential OFAC hit or match, you must do a little more research. The bureau resellers provide the SDN's last known demographic information that is available on OFAC's SDN list.

First, compare your customer's name to the name on the SDN list. How much of the SDN's name is matching against your customer's name? Are just one of two or more names matching (i.e., just the last name)?

If yes, you do not have a valid match and can proceed with the vehicle sale. Document the reason for moving on with the sale.

If you have an exact name match, compare the complete SDN entry with all the information you have on your customer. An SDN entry can have, for example, a full name, address, nationality, passport, tax ID, place of birth, date of birth, former names, and aliases. If you are missing a lot of this information for the name in your transaction, go back and get more information and then compare your complete information against the SDN entry.

If your information confirms that the person in your dealership is different from the person on the SDN list, go ahead and sell a vehicle. Document the steps taken to confirm your customer is not the same person on the SDN list.

If the information confirms that the person in your dealership is the same person on the SDN list, **you absolutely cannot sell a vehicle**. Instead, you must block the transaction and report the person to OFAC at 1-800-540-6322 or through the OFAC website.

How Do I Protect My Dealership?

While the risk that a terrorist is going to visit your dealership to buy a vehicle is likely slim, be mindful the SDN list also includes the terrorist's support staff, the drug dealers and money launderers that help fund terrorism. Profiling is not an acceptable approach to fulfill your obligation with OFAC's requirements.

The penalties for selling a car to someone on the OFAC list can be severe. Depending on the program, criminal penalties can include fines ranging from $50,000 to $10,000,000 and imprisonment ranging from 10 to 30 years for willful violations. Depending on the program, civil penalties range from $11,000 to $1,000,000 for each violation.

If you have concluded that the transaction in front of you is a false hit, document your conclusion on the media that shows you had a potential hit, place that information in the deal jacket or digital deal jacket, and proceed with the sale of the vehicle.

If you have a positive hit, document your blocked transaction confirmation to OFAC, including date, time, name of person you spoke with, and any instructions provided.

There is one final potential issue with a positive OFAC hit that can create litigation against your dealership. Under both the Fair Credit Reporting Act and the Equal Credit Opportunity Act, it is not a valid reason to deny a customer credit simply because they are on the OFAC list. You are not permitted to tell someone that they can't get approved for credit because they are on OFAC's list. OFAC provides guidance that you should tell the customer that you can't sell a vehicle to that customer because they are on the OFAC list and that the customer should contact OFAC directly.

Here's my take on the OFAC requirement – it is a pain in the backside – yet I shudder at the consequences of not blocking a transaction to any person, business, or country on the list. The process in a dealership has been extremely simplified with digital solutions. It only takes a few seconds to check, and a few minutes to document the false hit. Like it or not, the freedom we cherish has obligations. I have family members overseas serving their country; I have family members serving as law enforcement officials here. I am proud of both. Any little pain in the backside I endure to do my part is nothing compared to their commitment.

CHAPTER 16

Credit Scores and Deputy Dawg Duties

The Federales have deputized auto dealers to provide certain disclosures to consumers. Like it or not, retailers have an obligation to tell most of their customers what their credit score is.

In many cases, a dealer must disclose to the customer its credit score on either an Adverse Action Notice or on a Credit Score Disclosure Notice. Different Federal Laws mandate each requirement. The Adverse Action Notice can be required under either the Fair Credit Reporting Act or the Equal Credit Opportunity Act. Each Act provides a different trigger event to force the potential disclosure in the event an adverse action is taken.

The Credit Score Disclosure Notice is required under the Risk Based Pricing Rule and must be given to a consumer before he becomes obligated on a contract with a third-party finance source.

Adverse Action Notices

An adverse action is defined as:

"A refusal to grant credit in substantially the amount or on substantially the terms requested in an application unless the creditor makes a counteroffer (to grant credit in a different amount or on other terms), and the applicant uses or expressly accepts the credit offered."

The trigger event under the Fair Credit Reporting Act is the pulling of a credit bureau report. Conversely, when you accept a credit app from a consumer, you trigger a potential adverse action notification to the consumer under Reg B.

Although the law does not require a signature to pull a credit report, the creditor must be able to prove it had consent to pull a consumer's credit report. Most dealers require a signed credit application before pulling credit to have a defense when someone claims the dealer did not have permission to pull her or his credit.

As most dealers require a signed credit application before pulling credit, the trigger event for a potential adverse action notice becomes accepting a credit application under the Equal Credit Opportunity Act.

In *Imnotalawyer* terms, this essentially means if you accept a credit application, and do not sell the consumer a vehicle, you should provide the consumer with an Adverse Action Notice within 30 days of the receipt of the credit application.

Different Processes

There are different processes for providing an Adverse Action Notice in dealerships today. All processes rely upon a certain level of technology to at least print the Adverse Action Notice. And unlike the dealership I visited last year that had an IBM Selectric typewriter in the Accounting Office to process annual 1099s, nobody completes an Adverse Action Notice by hand.

Give it to Everyone

Some dealerships have a policy to give every consumer an Adverse Action Notice (and in many cases a Credit Score Disclosure Notice) as soon as a credit bureau report is pulled. The Dealer is taking a belt and suspender approach in that it cannot be sued for not providing an Adverse Action Notice. Some dealers also point out that they believe this process to be the least painless, require less thought by managers, less thought by its staff, and likely the most cost-efficient approach.

Those that disagree with this approach offer three arguments.

First, it potentially introduces a negative thought into the rapport building process of selling a vehicle and can raise an objection to overcome that is not necessary.

Second, some perceive a law that requires that something be done in certain circumstances means that it is only done when those certain circumstances materialize. In other words, you should only provide an Adverse Action Notice when an adverse action is taken.

Finally, the specter of a Dealer's agreement with the three Credit Reporting Agencies can come into play. Just like the Dealer-Lender Agreement outlines your responsibilities when assigning Retail Installment Contracts with the third-party finance source, each dealer has signed an agreement with each of the Credit Reporting Agencies.

The Credit Reporting Agencies are required to provide a free credit report to any consumer who has received an Adverse Action Notice who requests one. Credit Reporting Agencies do not like providing anything for free. A dealer who is giving every consumer it pulls a credit report on with an Adverse Action Notice is potentially increasing the Credit Reporting Agencies' costs. Rumors are that one of the Credit Reporting Agencies threatened a dealer with termination of its agreement if the dealer continued to provide Adverse Action Notices to all consumers it pulled a credit report on.

Send It to the Ones Who Don't Purchase

Other dealers take a more measured approach. They create a queue of consumers from whom they have accepted a credit application, filtered by date. If the consumers within a queue have not purchased a vehicle from the dealership within 15 days of the date of the credit application, an Adverse Action Notice is mailed.

Some of these dealers manage the process internally, with someone assigned the responsibility of checking the queue daily, confirming if the

145

consumer purchased a vehicle. If the consumer did not purchase a vehicle, the Adverse Action Notice is printed and mailed to the consumer.

Other dealers enlist the service of the vendor from whom it obtains the credit bureau report from. Most of these vendors will also create a queue, confirm that vehicle was not sold, print, and mail an Adverse Action Notice to the consumer. The cost for this service varies, so check with your credit bureau provider for its program and cost.

Those that prefer this approach believe that it filters out those consumers who purchase a vehicle from receiving an Adverse Action Notice and satisfies the requirement to send an Adverse Action Notice within 30 days of the adverse action.

Some dealers have adapted a hybrid process. In this hybrid, the credit bureau provider creates the queue. The dealer assigns a manager with the responsibility to clear out the queue on a periodic basis. This clearing action can be a combination of customers who did purchase a vehicle, or those customers who were eligible to purchase and finance a vehicle, but just could come to terms on color, or trade value, or price. The manager has the flexibility to remove anyone from the queue, then send a print request to the credit bureau provider for the notices to be printed. The provider will then print, stuff, and mail the Adverse Action Notices. These dealers feel that some of the consumers who were shopping two weeks ago may still be in the market. Sending an Adverse Action Notice at this point will tell the consumer that "We can't help you, so shop elsewhere."

Unwinds

Many of the cases I have worked as an expert witness involve a spot delivery gone bad. A common claim against the dealer in these cases is the lack of an Adverse Action Notice after the dealer repossessed the vehicle in the middle of the night.

Some dealers will send an Adverse Action Notice by certified mail on unwinds. Others will print an Adverse Action Notice, send it by regular mail, and document the file. Other dealers will simply worry about putting a for sale sign on the vehicle and not worry about an Adverse Action Notice.

Please don't be the third dealer.

Online Credit Applications

As dealers morph into the e-Dealership world, many of them are accepting credit applications online, either through a lead generator, the dealer's website, or other portals. Remembering that accepting a credit application is one of the trigger events that requires an AAN be sent within 30 days, the dealer should have a process to ensure that online credit applications become part of the queue to receive an AAN.

The Banks Send It So I don't Have To

I started helping dealers with their compliance initiatives just after the terrorist attacks on the twin towers in New York City, the Pentagon, and a farm field in Pennsylvania.

When the industry started its recovery and people were flying to other cities to start conducting business again, I started preaching that dealers were obligated to send Adverse Action Notices. Nearly every recap meeting included the objection "Our banks send that notice, we don't have to."

I've fought many compliance fights throughout the years, starting with Adverse Action Notices to clearing OFAC to Safeguards issues with copier machines to negative equity to cash back to customers to credit application manipulation to properly clearing Red Flags.

A dealer is a participating creditor in the indirect sales process by the fact that the dealer can establish the customer's APR. As such, the dealer is obligated to send its own Adverse Action Notice, and cannot rely on the finance source's Adverse Action notice.

Eventually (for the most part) our clients have come around to our position on these issues. Eventually, we have had to fire some clients who continued a path we could not sign off on. By now, all our clients are sending Adverse Action Notices. The variable is...which approach do they use.

Ultimately, once you realize you must have a process in place to provide an Adverse Action Notice, it becomes a business decision on which approach you decide on. Do you want to give an Adverse Action Notice to every consumer who walks through your doors? Do you want to send it two weeks later to those consumers who probably bought elsewhere? Or are you willing to take the risk of a lawsuit claiming you failed to send an Adverse Action Notice on a qualifying transaction?

It's a business decision.

Credit Score Disclosure Notices

The FTC finalized the Risk Based Pricing Notice in 2010, effective January 1, 2011. The underlying law is the FACT Act.

From the Rule: "The final rules generally require a creditor to provide a risk-based pricing notice to a consumer when the creditor uses a consumer report to grant or extend credit to the consumer on material terms that are materially less favorable than the most favorable terms available to a substantial proportion of consumers from or through that creditor."

The resulting requirement from the rule mean a dealer must provide a notice known as a Credit Score Disclosure Notice (CSDN) to the consumer that discloses the consumer's credit score and other disclosures. The intent of the Rule is to provide the consumer with information about his credit status before he commits to credit pricing and can therefore make an informed decision.

In 49 states, a dealer that pulls three credit bureaus only must disclose the score that was used primarily to determine the APR. In California, the scores for all bureaus that were pulled must be disclosed to the consumer.

Any consumer who finances or leases a vehicle through dealer sourced financing must receive a CSDN. This excludes outside lien and cash transactions.

The Rule does not require that the consumer sign the CSDN, but some vendors insert a signature line on the form, now making it a requirement to obtain the customer's signature.

The consumer should receive the CSDN when the score becomes available to the sales manager, but certainly must be given to the consumer before she signs a RISC or Lease Agreement. Like e-Desking, where I can review the timelines in the e-Desking software to ferret out payment packing, I can review the timeline in the credit application and credit bureau software to see when the CSDN was printed. This timeline will confirm if the process is being followed or if someone is breaking a Federal law by printing the CSDN days after the date of the contract.

Sometimes smart people in positions of authority make stupid decisions when they do not fully understand all the variables in a situation. Like a Sales Manager approving a deal when the sales person did not fully disclose the straw purchase. Or a father giving the OK to his daughter to spend the night with her friend Pat, which as it turns out, is short for Patrick. Or the Pentagon issuing late, conflicting guidance on the Military Lending Act that harms military personnel more than helps them.

The Federal Trade Commission (FTC) and a Federal Judge has apparently fallen into the same trap. Obviously smart people who made a stupid decision, to the detriment of car dealers.

At issue is the FTC's interpretation of a dealer's responsibility in providing notices to consumers as required by the Risk Based Pricing Rule. The FTC interprets the Risk Based Pricing Rule's use of the word "use" to mean that dealers must provide customers with a notice disclosing the customer's credit score, even if the dealer does not obtain a credit report itself.

The NADA sued the FTC and lost the first round in what promises to be a heavyweight fight with the FTC.

In what the NADA calls a flawed decision, and I call illogical to those of us who understand the business, the U.S. Court judge sided with the FTC's ruling that requires dealers to provide a notice to consumers even if the dealer does not pull a credit bureau report. The FTC illogically established a ruling that insists that since the dealer uses the credit score, it is the same as if the dealer pulled the credit report itself.

The NADA sued, arguing that the Rule did not contemplate the word "use" the same way the FTC interprets it in requiring a dealer to provide the notice if it simply passed the credit application along to a third-party lender.

Unfortunately, the judge disagreed with the NADA, who promises to appeal.

Until the appeal is heard, it certainly sounds like a dealer should provide a Credit Score Disclosure Notice to every customer it consummates a retail or lease deal with, even if the dealer did not pull a credit report.

Unfortunately, this means if you have been in the habit of submitting the credit app to the finance source and getting an approval before signing the customer up, you will need to get the credit score from the lender and generate a manual notice. Or (and like the NADA correctly points out), run the unnecessary expense of pulling a credit report just so that you can provide the notice before consummating the deal. Or a third option, and the cleanest, least costly option is to provide the customer with a "Score Unavailable" version of the CSDN.

Analog or Digital

Perhaps because the Risk Based Pricing Rule became a requirement during the internet age, or because the credit bureau providers quickly gave dealers an option to print the CSDN at the same time the credit bureau is printed, I do not know of a single dealer who is attempting to manage the CSDN process manually. Not even the dealer who still has a working IBM Selectric typewriter in the Accounting Office to manually type 1099s.

Essentially, every consumer who completes a credit application with the dealership should receive a notice disclosing her credit score. If she submits a credit application and does not purchase a vehicle, an Adverse Action Notice should be sent within 30 days. The consumer's credit score is one of the disclosures on the AAN. If he submits a credit application and purchases and finances a vehicle, he must receive a Credit Score Disclosure Notice, which discloses his credit score.

CHAPTER 17

Used Vehicles

Motorcycle dealers can skip this chapter. You are exempt from the FTC Used Car Rule, don't have to book out your bikes for your finance sources, and I can't recall the last motorcycle recall.

For the rest of you – I've carved out this chapter because of the nuances of selling and financing used vehicles that do not exist in the new car building. Some of the used vehicle specific requirements include: Used Car Buyer's Guides; prior history or damage disclosures; and branded or salvage titling. Used vehicles do share the onus of recalls with their new vehicle brethren.

Used Car Buyer's Guides

The FTC issued the Used Car Rule in 1985 and dealers immediately started messing up the required disclosures on the Used Car Guide. This Guide is the labeling requirement from the Rule and is intended to provide consumers with any remaining warranty information. The Guide must be posted on all used vehicles and demonstrators available for sale, so the consumer can have the information available as she is making the purchase decision.

In 2017, the guide was revised to accommodate industry changes. In 1985, there were no such things as Certified Pre-Owned programs sponsored by the manufacturers. There were no air bags. No one had an email address.

The revised Guide incorporated these new items. And again, dealers immediately started messing up the required disclosures.

The Used Car Rule is the only Federal law or rule governing our industry that requires a Spanish translation of the form if the deal was negotiated in part in Spanish. Some cities and states have foreign language requirements. If you negotiate a deal in Polish in Chicago, you must have the customer sign a Polish Language Translation Form and give the customer a Polish language RISC. California law requires that a Foreign Language Disclosure form be signed, and an accompanying foreign translation RISC given to the customer if the transaction was negotiated in one of five non-English languages. But the Used Car Rule is the only Federal law requiring a foreign language translation.

Of all the forms that we review in a deal file review, this single form is the one most often incorrectly completed. So do the Federales. Just ask the Arkansas dealer who was fined $80,000 b the FTC for not having the Guide on all their used vehicles.

The Analog Process

Some dealers continue to order three-ply forms and have a lot porter handwrite the disclosure information on the form. Some dealers use a stamp to stamp the warranty information on the form, but do not always stamp each of the three plies. The lot porter then tapes the three-ply form to the back window, or maybe not. Usually, this handwritten, analog form is not properly completed. There are occasions when the form is ripped in a test drive and not replaced. There are other dealers who require the F&I Manager print the form in F&I, and the warranty disclosed on the vehicle can be different than the warranty printed in F&I and given to the customer.

The Digital Process

Other dealers either hire a franchised vendor to manage the Used Car Guides on the used vehicles, or purchase software to print the guides and have a lot porter post them in the vehicles. One of the pitfalls with the digital process using a vendor is when a used vehicle makes its way to the lot out of PDI and the vendor only comes twice a week. This potentially leaves a vehicle available for sale without the required guide posted in the window. Just as with the analog process, when the F&I Manager is tasked with printing the guide in F&I, there may be conflicting warranty information between two forms.

Prior History or Damage Disclosure

I'm not aware of any Federal requirement to disclose prior history or damage on a used vehicle, but there are requirements in many states to disclose prior history or damage with more joining the list. Some states have forms the customer must sign disclosing any one of 21 potential prior uses, while other states have a few prior uses such as demonstrators that are disclosed on the Buyer's Order.

States such as Indiana require the disclosure of previous material damage, while Colorado's prior damage disclosure is better defined and a little more stringent.

Dealers can struggle with these disclosure requirements through a lack of knowledge, but unfortunately, that is not an adequate defense against claims of non-disclosure.

The analog approach is to have a manager inspect every used vehicle offered for sale, regardless of sourcing, looking for signs or evidence of prior damage. This may or may not work, depending on the quality of the fix her up job. It certainly does not ascertain prior use. To determine prior use in an analog process, the dealer either knows that it purchased the vehicle from a rental car company, or knows it was a dealer demonstrator, or guesses.

Digitally, dealers can rely somewhat on available software solutions, such as CARFAX or Auto Check. We advise our clients to print the CARFAX or

Auto Check report on the date of delivery, have the customer sign a copy for the file, and give the customer a separate copy. Since there is often a delay in reporting prior damage or usage with these vendors, printing one on the date of delivery is critical. This potentially gives the dealer defense that, to the best of his knowledge, using an industry recognized independent source, the dealer disclosed known prior damage or use.

Branded or Salvage Titles

When a car has been in an accident, flood, hail, vandalism, or auto theft in some states, and the amount of the damage exceeds a high percent of the vehicle's value, an insurance company will declare the vehicle a total loss. The next step will vary by state, with many states issuing a salvage title.

There are facilities that specialize in purchasing these vehicles and repair them for resale. Most states will then issue a branded title after the vehicle passes a safety inspection.

Many dealers shy away from selling salvage or branded title vehicles. Many states require that the seller disclose a branded title vehicle during the sale. A California statute requires dealers to post a big neon sticker on the window of any used vehicle with a branded title. I have yet to see a big neon sticker on any used vehicle in California...because they don't sell vehicles with branded titles.

There is software available to vet a vehicle for a branded title. CARFAX and Auto Check are two.

A National Motor Vehicle Title Information System (NMVTIS) report is required on every used vehicle offered for sale in California. This service is available for dealers in other states (www.vehiclehistory.gov). The power of this vender's report is that state titling agencies, insurance carriers, auto recyclers, junk, and salvage yards are required to regularly report vehicle information to NMVTIS.

Recall

As cars have moved from crank windows to power windows, from 8-tracks to DVRs and TVs, the electronics and sophistication have escalated. So too have failure rates of these sensitive switches and connections.

Add to that the change in many manufacturers' attitudes about recalls. With crank windows and 8-tracks the attitude was to suppress recalls for fear of showing weakness in building a faulty vehicle. The press coverage was ominous. Messrs. Cronkite and Brinkley would lead their newscasts with the bad news for a week before disclosing how many soldiers were killed that week in the Vietnam War.

After a few governments intervened and hit some manufacturers with huge fines, attitudes changed. Now recalls are a non-event from a newscaster's view. Not so with the Federales, though. The FTC has ruled that if a dealer is selling a vehicle as "Certified", the dealer must correct any recalls if it is the dealer's brand or inform the consumer of the incurred recall if it is not the dealer's brand.

Recalls, however, are not necessarily a non-event in the world of auto sales. New Car Sales Managers and many sales people know what recalls are open on their inventory. They know which vehicles have stop sales.

Used vehicles can pose different issues. Say your dealership has the big blue oval as its sign. You sell some used Fords and are likely aware of any recalls.

What about the Toyota SUV? Or the Chevy sedan? Or the BMW crossover?

If you must disclose recalls in your state, or even if you don't but do because it's good business, how are you to know about recalls on vehicles from manufacturers whose new vehicles are sold by another dealer?

Most dealers rely on either the CARFAX or Auto Check report. This is another reason printing a copy on the date of delivery and retaining the copy with the customer's signature is important.

But - what if you fixed the recall or had the dealer down the street fix the recall and it is still in the CARFAX or Auto Check report as an open recall? Unfortunately, these reports are not updated in real time.

There is another government website to the rescue. www.safercar.gov is a website that is more current on cleared recalls than are CARFAX and Auto Check. Many dealers have established a Dealer Law requiring that a printout from the website, signed by the customer, showing an all clear is completed on every vehicle transaction. The FTC requires a copy of this report be given to the consumer if the dealer is labeling a used vehicle that is not the dealer's brand as "Certified" and the dealer has not fixed the recall.

Used vehicles are a profitable piece of a successful dealer's portfolio. Following the required disclosure requirements as imposed by the Federales will help a dealer keep that profit in the bank, not transfer it to the Dark Side.

CHAPTER 18

The Case for Training and Industry Certification

"December 7, 1941, a day that will live in infamy."
- *Franklin Roosevelt*
"December 7, 2017, a watershed moment in American culture."
- *Me*

Pearl Harbor was bombed in 1941, effectively bringing America into World War II.

Senator Al Franken resigned his congressional seat on December 7, 2017, joining a list of 100 or so men to that point who have been publicly accused of sexual harassment. The revelations of sexual harassment charges have hit a broad spectrum of professions, including political, entertainment, sports, business, and news agencies.

Some of the accused in Congress are facing ethics hearings. Men in other professions are facing public humiliation, loss of business, or careers.

This is not about the politics of sexual harassment. Or taking any side about accuser and accused.

Rather, it is about one of the very real requirements for businesses, including dealers and F&I agencies, to annually provide ongoing training in five critical areas: Sexual Harassment, Ethics, Discrimination, Safeguards, and Red Flags.

Sexual Harassment

Sexual harassment is against the law and has no place in a dealership. Employees, managers, customers, and vendors are potential victims of sexual harassment.

The two specific types of sexual harassment are quid pro quo and hostile environment.

Quid pro quo is the type of sexual harassment that is generating today's headlines. It simply means that someone in a position of power over another person engages in unwelcome sexual advances, requests for sexual favors, and other sexually-related conduct in exchange for job or other benefits.

It can be man on woman, man on man, woman on man, or woman on woman.

Sexual harassment also exists if the conduct creates a hostile work environment or intolerable working conditions. Examples include posters, jokes, suggestive music, whistles, etc.

Engaging in sexual harassment can result in discipline, public embarrassment, or termination, and expose a dealership to legal liability.

If you become aware of, or even suspect, any form of sexual harassment at a dealership, it should immediately be reported to management or owners.

To provide the underpinnings of a potential defense against charges of sexual harassment, a dealership should document that initial and annual sexual harassment training has been completed for all employees.

Ethics

Ethics really boils down to the Golden Rule: *Do Unto Others as You Would Have Them Do Unto You.*

For example, if you would be comfortable with a sales manager packing the payment on your grandma's next vehicle purchase, you might have a problem with your moral compass. Or grandma can't cook.

Just like sexual harassment, ethics seems so simple, yet is very complex. Documentation of annual training on ethics may help provide a defense against potential claims.

Discrimination

The law prohibits not only intentional discrimination (disparate treatment), but also prohibits facially neutral policies or actions that disproportionately negative effect on a protected class of persons and are not defensible as having a legitimate business purpose that cannot be accomplished by other means (disparate impact).

The law also prohibits employment decisions based on: stereotypes and assumptions about abilities, traits, or the performance of individuals of certain groups.

It's illegal to discriminate against any individual regarding employment. Dealerships should adopt policies to reduce the likelihood of discrimination.

If racial information is needed, to simultaneously guard against discriminatory selection, use separate forms or otherwise keep the information about an applicant's race separate from the application.

Hostile work environments or harassment on the job are prohibited.

Dealerships are required to take appropriate steps to prevent and correct unlawful harassment.

As with sexual harassment, documentation of annual training of all employees on the dealer's discrimination policy could help defend or deflect charges of employee discrimination.

Safeguards Rule

Safeguards is all about treating customers' non-public, personal information (NPI) as if it were your information. Chances are with all the recent security breaches; your information is already on the Dark Web. As a dealer, you have lists and other consumer NPI that you are responsible for safeguarding.

An annual training program for all employees in the Dealer's Safeguards program should be part of the program's guidelines.

Red Flags Rule

A Red Flag is a pattern, practice or activity which signals the potential risk of identity theft. Some examples include altered or forged identification documents, address discrepancies, Social Security Number discrepancies, alerts in credit bureaus, or driver's license descriptions that don't match the appearance of the person presenting it.

The Red Flags Rule requires an annual report to the owner of the business regarding the sufficiency of the business' red flags program. Part of that annual report should be certification that annual training has been provided to all employees on the business' Red Flags Program.

Many Human Resource Managers are aware of the need to provide annual training in these critical areas. Automotive Compliance Education (ACE) believes it is so critical to a dealer's defense against potential claims that these five components are required modules in the ACE certified practitioner's annual re-certification.

We are an industry of business professionals. Salespeople know more about the features and benefits of the vehicles they sell than the average citizen. Sales and F&I Managers know how to calculate monthly payments for retail and leases while many consumers would struggle to do so.

Like other industries filled with professionals, we have our share of kinks. Lawyers are disbarred. Doctors are stripped of their licenses. Teachers can no longer teach. CPAs stop counting. No industry is without its bad seeds.

Our industry differs from the other professional industries in that we do not require an Industry Certification or Continued Education. Lawyers, Physicians, Nurses, Dentists, Teachers, and CPAs must pass a test to become certified or licensed. They must also demonstrate continual learning in their field to maintain their certification or license. Not surprisingly, these professions are among the top ten most trusted professions according to the latest Gallup poll that measures such things.

ACE Certification and Continuing Education

My fellow members at White Hawk Country Club have engaged in a conversation that I am sure goes one at every golf course in America. It seems that some members always win the money events because we believe they sandbag their handicap. For the non-golfers, a handicap is an algorithm that takes the scores from your last twenty rounds of golf and delivers a number between zero (scratch golfer) and 40 (usually a beginner). This handicap is used to even the playing field in matches and tournaments. Some golfers are suspected of posting higher that actual scores for a round of golf, or conveniently forgetting to post lower scores. This give them an artificially high handicap, which benefits them in matches and tournaments that use the net score (the score after you subtract your handicap from your actual). For example, if you shoot an 80 in a tournament, and have a 15 handicap, you will have a net score of 65. Par on most courses is between 70 and 72, so a score of 65 is greatly under par, and likely to win a match or tournament.

As the group is lamenting the effect of sandbaggers in a recent members' meeting and offering solutions that the club pro should take to address the issue, he reminded us of a simple fact.

Golf is a game of honor and *You Cannot Legislate Honesty*.

So true in golf and in our industry. We can still try, though.

Automotive Compliance Education (ACE) to the rescue. ACE provides seven different curricula for the automotive industry professional, depending upon the level of responsibility in the dealership or vendors serving the industry.

The curricula range from two hours of online training for the Sales Person and BDC staff to 15 hours of modules delivered online for the Company Compliance Officer. Curricula for the Sales Manager, Office Manager, Compliance Clerk, F&I Manager, and Product Specialist take between two to ten hours to complete.

After completing the course work, the student takes an exam to confirm a legitimate level of understanding of the curriculum and is certified.

More importantly, the certified professional is required to complete a shorter course load as part of the continuing education process. The courses include required annual training such as Ethics, Discrimination, Harassment, Safeguards, and Red Flags. Additional training is provided for any new topics since the professional was last certified. Finally, any gvo3 & Associates' client is retrained on audit failure points from the last compliance review.

Potential Whistle Blower Defense

One huge benefit to the Dealer Principal and HR Professional is a potential defense against a whistle blower's claim that the dealer did not provide training. After all, the dealer recognized that the industry is heavily regulated and decided to provide compliance training for the employee. The employee undertakes the training and successfully passes a test demonstrating a command of the topic. After the certification, the employee's work output is audited, and failure points are uncovered. The employee is then retrained on the failure points and passes another test.

The employee has a shaky case alleging that the Dealer failed to provide training in this critical area.

Afterword

Hopefully you enjoyed the read and the war stories and the compliance discussions. I also hope that you read something, the light went on, and you mumbled "Hmmmm."

This is the current reporting of today's environment and the approaches dealers are leveraging to both protect themselves against Dark Side attacks and to transition their business from pulp to ions.

Five years from now, there will be new compliance requirements and new Dealer Laws will be developed. Continue reading and learning and absorbing so you can stay successful.

Good Luck and Good Selling.